family under construction

family under construction

building relationships with those who matter most

by
Walter Hallam

Harrison House
Tulsa, Oklahoma

Family Under Construction:
Building Relationships With Those Who Matter Most
ISBN 1-57794-191-8
Copyright © 1999 by Walter Hallam
P. O. Box 1515
LaMarque, TX 77568

Published by Harrison House, Inc.
P. O. Box 35035
Tulsa, OK 74153

contents

Introduction 7

Part 1—Marriage: A Covenant Relationship 11

  1 A Match Made in Heaven 13

  2 A Covenant Marriage: Anointed Wine From God . .35

  3 God's Mantle for the Family 53

Part 2—Men Are Tupperware, Women Are China 63

  4 Superglue for Your Relationship 65

  5 Tupperware Versus China 77

  6 Women: The Finer Things in Life 89

  7 Foundations for a Godly Home 103

Part 3—Three Lifelines in Marriage 113

  8 Lifeline #1: Communication 115

  9 Lifeline #2: Sex and Intimacy 127

  10 Lifeline #3: Finances 141

Part 4—The Ministry of a Family 157

  11 Developing a Strong Family 159

  12 Raising Children God's Way 171

  13 Turning Hearts Toward Home 181

introduction

Jamie walked through the front door of the house after a long day of work. Her mind mulled over the events of the day. Her boss, Mr. Reese, had given her an impossible deadline; and, though Jamie had neglected all of her other responsibilities and had even skipped lunch, she had been unable to finish the project on time. When she had walked into her boss's office to hand in the project, an hour late, he frowned, not even responding to her heartfelt apology.

Now, finally at home, Jamie longed for a quiet place to calm her raging emotions.

"Hi, Jamie. What are we having for supper tonight?" Jamie heard her husband, Mark, say as she walked into the living room.

Mark had been reading in his chair since he had arrived home, fifteen minutes before, from a very demanding day at work. He was trying to drown out the sounds in his memory of angry customers' voices on the phone and thoughts of upcoming deadlines.

Jamie noticed that he didn't even looked up to address her. He was sitting on his recliner, shuffling through pages of the newspaper.

"I don't feel like cooking tonight," she said.

"Do you want to order out?" Mark asked, still shuffling through the paper.

"Whatever you want is fine," Jamie said, fuming inside because of Mark's seeming lack of concern for her. "Why don't you fix yourself something or order out or whatever you want? I'm going to bed. I'm tired."

Looking up from the paper, Mark suddenly realized that Jamie was distressed. Wanting to comfort her, he asked, "What's wrong, Jamie?"

She proceeded to tell him about the difficult day she'd had.

"Jamie," Mark said, "you just need to talk to Mr. Reese tomorrow." He was upset that Jamie had been treated with such disrespect. "Tell him you did not appreciate his failure to acknowledge your hard work."

"I can't talk to Mr. Reese, Mark. He would never listen."

"Then why don't you quit? You have so many skills; you could find a much better job, Jamie. You need to work for someone who appreciates your talent and hard work."

"You know I love my position at work. I don't want to quit. I just..." Jamie paused in frustration. "I don't need you to solve this for me, Mark." She heard the volume of her voice unintentionally rising.

Mark stood, shocked, feeling rejected and not knowing what to say.

Many times we all struggle to reach out and connect with the people who matter the most to us, but unfortunately, we don't always know the best way to do that. Whether it's a spouse, a child, a coworker or a family member, sometimes we need help in building the bridges that will carry us across the streams of disappointment and struggle, to stand on the solid ground of understanding and acceptance.

But how do we get to the other side of miscommunication and disappointment when our thoughts and methods of communication and caring are so different?

Men are like Tupperware, and women are like china. Both can perform similar functions, to a degree. But their presentation or expression of that function is completely different. And, quite frankly, that's the way it should be. But such differences can pose a challenge, and, if not perceived correctly, these differences can result in creating a deeper rift rather than constructing a bridge.

We can't always understand one another, and our differences often pull us apart. But our differences can pull us together—if we can recognize and appreciate them.

In every relationship we have, we need to learn how to use our differences for *construction*—for building each other up—instead of for *destruction*. And the best way to learn about our differences and how to use them for construction is to look to the One who created our differences. God cares about the relationships we have with others—with spouses, children, siblings, parents, coworkers and friends.

In this book, we will explore God's thoughts about, and purposes for, the most important relationships in our lives. If you have been facing the frustration of misunderstood differences, or if you just want to find out how to become a more unified family, consider some of the proven tools and techniques

I've discovered that will help you build satisfying and lasting relationships with the people who matter the most.

—*Pastor Walter Hallam*
LaMarque, Texas

Part I

Marriage:
A Covenant
Relationship

a match made in heaven

Anyone who is married knows that marriage brings many changes. So if you're not married and want to be, get ready! Change will definitely come your way, and it will stretch you as well as your mate-to-be. Change will dispel any unrealistic notions you ever had regarding marriage.

I believe there are three reasons why people marry. The predominant reason I believe people get married is *physical* attraction. The second reason is what I call *soulish* attraction. The third reason—and I trust this is your reason—is *spiritual* attraction.

Physical attraction is really quite simple. It says, "My flesh likes your flesh. My eyes like what they see. I look at you, I like you and I want you." When people are motivated by outward appearance only, they tend to develop a relationship based on what they want, their own selfishness. And in today's society that's the big thing.

sex! sex! sex!

Have you ever noticed how sex sells everything? You can't even buy chewing gum without somebody half-clothed trying to sell it! People become physically attracted to each other predominantly because they have been inundated with that particular marketing technique. The lust of the flesh, the lust of the eyes and the pride of life is big business today.

We are living with a generation of young people today who have grown into adulthood learning to base their attraction to a man or a woman on the sexual potential they think is in a relationship. But unfortunately, when people marry merely because of physical attraction, they usually end up divorced.

About half of all marriages end in divorce within the first two years. That's not to say the reason people get divorced is simply because the physical attraction has lost its pizazz. The reason is that most people marry in the flesh. They marry because of what they see in the natural—money, security or beauty.

Even though these qualities do have merit, these things alone are very unsatisfying and unfulfilling in life. In time the other cares of life will override any seasonal pleasures those natural qualities once brought.

water buffaloes and tick birds

The second reason that people are predominantly attracted to one another and fall in love is soulish attraction. Soulish attraction means that we are on basically the same intellectual level—we enjoy a lot of the same interests in life. One person who likes ice cream may meet someone who also likes ice cream and say, "We should get married because we have so much in common!" A couple may like a particular kind of music or have similar hobbies. It's *almost* a match made in heaven. The only problem is that it isn't necessarily a match made in heaven. Why? Because the older you get and the older your family gets, the more everyone changes.

Have you ever noticed that the things you liked when you were eighteen just don't appeal to you as much anymore? At the moment someone falls in love with a man or woman, he or she may have a soulish attraction to that person. But I promise you that the older he or she gets, the more those same interests may grow further apart.

So if you're marrying someone based upon the fact that you have a lot in common, that marriage could be headed for some very rocky times ahead when things change. You can't treat your spouse right now like you did when you were eighteen, twenty or twenty-five. If you're trying to treat him or her like the eighteen-, twenty- or twenty-five-year-old you married, it's amazing how your spouse won't yield to that any longer—he or she grew up!

You don't stop growing just because you reach the legal voting age; you continue to develop and mature as a person. You pick up new perspectives and drop off outdated views that once appealed to you.

When I was a child growing up, my mother couldn't get me to eat cauliflower, and you'd have to call the National Guard to get me to eat broccoli. When my mother would cook foods like steamed or boiled cabbage, I tell you, there was just something about it that would make me totally reject the stuff. If Mama put it on the table, my stomach would hurt! If she said, "You have to eat this before you can leave the table," I would be there for what seemed to me like days!

Today, here I am at a ripe "young" age and holding, and it's incredible how much I like broccoli. I can make a meal on veggies. And I love hot, steamed cabbage with a little bit of bacon!

Some time ago I was watching a documentary on TV about water buffaloes. These water buffaloes had little birds on their backs called tick birds. The water buffalo and tick bird don't have much fellowship—there's very little communication between the two of them. But they do have a unique social relationship. The water buffalo is like a two-ton plate, and the tick bird sits on top of his back eating all the ticks he wants. It keeps the water buffalo well-groomed in the process, and the bird gets fed himself. So they have this social relationship—it's good for the buffalo and it's good for the tick bird.

Now, let's be honest. Many marriages are simply social arrangements like that of the water buffalo and the tick bird. The husband comes in from a long day, sits down at the table and grunts, "Biscuits, cornbread, fried chicken." Then he gets up from the table, wobbles into the living room, plops down on the couch and lies there for approximately twelve hours until he goes to work the next day. If he's not a snorer, the wife gets a mirror and holds it under his nose to see if his breath fogs it up. Sure enough, he's still alive.

Mama, in the meantime, is happy just to get him out of her hair. When he walks in the door, her usual questions are, "Do you have the check? Can we pay the bills?"

"Huh?" is the usual response, because by this time of the day, he's brain-dead.

So she takes the paycheck, gives him the stub, and what happens to it beyond that is never discussed—unless they're running a little short.

That's when the water buffalo grunts. "Hey, I want to talk to you a minute. How come there's no money in the checking account?" he says.

"Why don't you make more?" the tick bird replies.

God didn't call us *just* to have a social arrangement in marriage, like two ships passing in the night, occasionally seeing one another. A social relationship and a sexual relationship should be healthy by-products of the true marriage relationship: a spiritual relationship.

united in love

The best and only God-sanctioned level of marital attraction is spiritual attraction. Spiritual attraction is the level of attraction where *God* puts two people together. This is when He begins to cause the spirits and hearts of these two people to be drawn to one another in a relationship that's not built upon their fleshly desires.

Before they're married, people have no way of knowing if God is directing them toward marriage if they yield to the desires of the flesh. When you're listening to pride and lust, it is impossible to hear the voice of God clearly. His priorities for you in a marriage partner may seem to be different from what the world may see as important, but His direction is the first thing you should seek.

You may have a list of qualities you are seeking in a mate, and you may be checking it twice. But if the last one on your list has something to do with church, you are heading for a world of hurt. The number one thing you should be concerned about when seeking a mate is whether or not the person you plan to marry loves God and is full of the Holy Ghost.

Another question you should consider is whether God wants your involvement with another person to be on any other level than a spiritual relationship or just to remain a friendship. Begin to say to yourself, *I refuse to give myself to anybody on any level, except those whom God approves.* That's how you will find a wife or a husband from the Lord.

The Spirit of God may reveal someone to you, but that revelation doesn't necessarily mean that you should go get married tomorrow! There's no such thing as love at first sight. You may know by the Spirit of God that He has spoken to you about an individual, but you won't fall in love at first sight, no matter what your soulish feelings may tell you. That is just a poetic fable that isn't in line with the Word of God.

Any love relationship of the Spirit needs an "incubation period," a time to develop. Even though you may see some-one and think, *Wow! This is it!* in your spirit, it still takes time to develop a true and lasting love. A love relationship of the Spirit takes time to develop as a spiritual attraction.

If you're single and you want to be married or even if you are planning to be married soon, try this test on your future mate. Take that girl or guy to church with you. Take them to a singles' ministry fellowship. Take them to the next crusade.

Take them to a prayer group. Get some other couples who are full of the Holy Ghost and go out as one big group.

That's right. If you feel like God's in it, honey, you need to take him where God is. Observe how he worships and praises God. See if his heart gets offended because you want to go to church. And don't listen to come-on's like, "Instead of being in church, I'd just rather be alone with you. I can hear God better when I'm with you." If he ever tells you that, just reply to him, "Well, you don't need me until you can hear God without me!" The same is true for that woman you have your sights set on, men!

A spiritual relationship is a relationship where, first of all, two people love Jesus Christ. Two hearts blend together as their ambitions become one. Their destinies are so entwined that there aren't enough demons in hell or people on the planet to tear them apart. They have made a decision to be faithful and loyal to God as a family unit and to one another all of their lives. It's where two people have *agape* (unconditional) love ruling their thoughts and minds. Selfishness and hardness of heart are weeded out and replaced with a desire to please God and each other.

In a spiritual relationship, the husband and wife aren't trying to see how much time they can spend apart without making the other angry. They're not embarrassed or ashamed to pray together. Instead, they look for ways to be together.

I look for ways to be with my wife, Cindy, and I've asked God to teach me how to be a good husband. Working together, God and Cindy are training me to be a good husband. Sometimes I'll call Cindy and say, "Honey, have you eaten lunch yet?" If she hasn't, then I'll say, "Well, it'll take me about thirty minutes to pick you up. If you can wait for me, I'll take you to lunch." I'm constantly looking for ways to be around my wife, not for ways to avoid her, because I like everything about her. I especially like the way she smells when she puts on her favorite perfume. It makes me think, *Man! She's still got it.* The more I look for ways to be with Cindy, the stronger our spiritual relationship, which bonds our hearts together, becomes.

God's righteous family

The first chapter of Matthew shows how righteousness enters the family relationship when Jesus is made the center of it. Through the marriage of Joseph and Mary, and the virgin birth of Jesus, God reversed every curse that had followed mankind from the Garden of Eden. He reversed the curses of strife, envy, disbelief, disobedience and hardness of heart. For every family who puts Jesus in the center of their home, the curse is reversed.

When Jesus is the center of a marriage, there's a chance for a powerful relationship to exist. It requires a servant's heart to maintain the character of godliness inside the four walls of a home. The Bible says Jesus humbled Himself and took upon Himself the form of a servant. He *served* His way right into the power of resurrection!

If you want to see resurrection power bring life to a dying marital relationship, begin by serving one another. Even if your mate isn't willing to serve you, make every effort to serve him or her with all your heart. Sooner or later a ripple effect will take place. Your mate will begin to recognize Jesus in you. When the kids see Mom and Dad serving one another with humble hearts, they'll begin to react differently. When children see their parents draw closer to each other, they will feel more secure.

God puts men and women together to reveal Himself to the world. In Matthew 1, we see how God joined Joseph and Mary to reveal Himself to you. I've outlined six areas that were necessary to their spiritual life and which are vital to marriages today.

1. Salvation of both spouses

If you're going to have a spiritual relationship in marriage, the first thing you need to do, my friend, is to get saved from your sins.

It is impossible for two people to have a spiritual home if one mate is a believer and the other isn't. Now, that doesn't mean you're not truly married. But your relationship will be lacking in the sense that a spiritual person can never be understood by a person who isn't born again and filled with the Spirit of God. It is absolutely impossible to understand the ways of the Spirit with the natural mind.

That's the reason your mate can't understand why you want to go to church so much. It's not because your spouse is a mean or bad person. It's just that he or she can't understand the ways of the Spirit or understand why you want to be in God's house. To the unsaved, church is a foreign place!

Do these questions sound familiar? "Why can't you just recite the rosary or say a few 'Our Fathers' or something?" "Why do you always have to speak in that strange language?" "Why do you sing those same songs over and over again? I don't understand."

Having a truly spiritual relationship with your marriage partner begins by both of you being born again and filled with the Spirit of God. Your minds are renewed to the ways of the Spirit as you grow together in your walk with the Lord.

2. *Spirit-to-Spirit Communication* good!

In a spiritual relationship, you have to develop communication between your spirits, not just flesh-to-flesh or mind-to-mind communication. Men, decide that your communication with your wife won't be based on what you can get out of her or what she can do for you, but upon her honor as a woman of God.

When we begin to communicate spirit-to-spirit, we will see our spouses as the most anointed people we know. Sometimes people think, *Oh, if I can just get the pastor to lay hands on me, the anointing will flow and I'll be healed.*

Well, honey, the pastor may be gone tomorrow. Then what are you going to do? Wake up and smell the coffee! You've got somebody right next to you who is full of the Holy Ghost. Tell your husband or wife, "Sweetheart, put your hands on me and pray. I see and respect the Spirit of God in you." First Peter 3:7 says that if we get in agreement, our prayers will not be hindered. So learn to communicate spirit-to-spirit.

A pastor who operates in the prophetic anointing may speak a word to you, saying, "Thus saith the Lord...," and you take it as a word from God. But if your husband or wife has a word from the Lord, you just yawn or take it lightly. The Bible says, **Despise not prophesyings** (1 Thess. 5:20). This verse doesn't say, "Despise not prophesying if it comes from the pastor." God may use the person closest to you to speak His Word into your life, and you would miss it!

Watch out for negative pronouncements over your marriage, such as: "Oh, if my husband would just prophesy like the pastor does." Or, "Oh, if my wife just sang like the church soloist. My, would we have a powerful relationship." Forget it! Learn to honor and respect the move of God at work right now in your mate. God took the two of you and made you one. So learn to live with yourself!

One of the main reasons people don't communicate spirit-to-spirit in a marriage relationship is that they associate their own spiritual weaknesses with their spouses'. They don't realize the person God has raised up to complement them is living *with them*. Learn to communicate spirit-to-spirit and allow God to move through your spouse to strengthen your weaknesses and build you up. AmEN!

3. *Find your divine destiny in God*

Every home has an ultimate destiny. No matter what you think, you're not married just to put in eight hours at the office, bring home a paycheck, lie around the house, kick back, get eight hours of sleep at night and then go back to the office the next day. That's not the call of God on your life. God has a higher purpose for a man and a woman.

In Deuteronomy 32:30 God says that one can chase a thousand and two can put ten thousand to flight. That means if God is their God, and a man and woman have a spiritual marriage relationship, then there's an army living in their house. There's a purpose for their marriage. So begin to seek God now for your divine destiny and develop it in your marriage relationship.

Let's look at the lives of God's New Testament family—Mary and Joseph. Mary and Joseph thought they were just two good Jewish people who were about to be married. They looked forward to having a house full of kids, bar mitzvahs and a lifetime of memories. Little did they know that God had something far greater for them to do. One day, following their betrothal, Gabriel appeared to Mary. Some time later Joseph had a dream. They eventually found themselves leaving Bethlehem—the only home they'd known—and living in Egypt, running from the king who tried to assassinate their son. Although in the natural it may have appeared strange, in the Spirit Mary and Joseph were following the plan of God.

Following the plan of God is *exciting*—the Holy Ghost just may call you into the ministry. Little did my wife and I know what would happen to us when we were called into full-time ministry. We had our own plans—I wanted to be a millionaire and a deacon (in that order) and was pressing toward that goal as rapidly as I knew how. I was working until my brains were oozing out of my ears! I was busy working on my own destiny, tithing, offering, making money, being a good man and serving God. Little did I know that one day God would interrupt my life and say, "Quit your job and everything you're doing. Get ready because I'm going to launch you into the world for My service."

I had a choice. I could either keep making money, or I could start preaching the gospel. I decided to preach. Cindy and I talked about it. We knew in our spirits that this was from God, so we made the decision to pursue God's divine destiny for us.

Your personal ambition may be from God; and if it is, continue following Him. But if it's not, make the decision to find your divine destiny as a husband and wife by together making Jesus the center of your home. Perhaps you've been saying, "My spouse absolutely will not have anything to do with it. He'll leave me; I know it." Hardness of heart will run an unbeliever one of two ways: to the altar or to the woods! So if you follow the call of God that's upon your home, your spouse will do one of two things: get in or get out.

Never forget that the first person you are "married" to is Jesus of Nazareth. No other man or woman has died for you, and no one—absolutely no one—needs to keep you from going to heaven. But don't go out and get rid of your spouse just because he or she is an unbeliever. First, get Jesus in the middle of your home; then begin to develop the divine call of God in your relationship.

Find and develop your divine destiny and purpose. For that to take place, you will have to lay down your own life. Ephesians 5:21-33 is very clear about the roles of husbands and wives in developing divine destiny:

Submitting yourselves one to another in the fear of God. Wives, submit yourselves unto your own husbands, as unto the Lord. For the husband is the head of the wife, even as Christ is the head of the church: and he is the saviour of the body. Therefore as the church is subject unto Christ, so let the wives be to their own husbands in every thing. Husbands, love your wives, even as Christ also loved the church, and gave himself for it; That he might sanctify and cleanse it with the washing of water by the word, That he might present it to himself a glorious church, not having spot, or wrinkle, or any such thing; but that it should be holy and without blemish. So ought men to love their wives as their own bodies. He that loveth his wife loveth himself. For no man ever yet hated his own flesh, but nourisheth and cherisheth it, even as the Lord the church: For we are members of his body, of his flesh, and of his bones. For this cause shall a man leave his father and mother, and shall be joined unto his wife, and they two shall be one flesh. This is a great mystery: but I speak concerning Christ and the church. Nevertheless let every one of you in particular so love his wife even as himself; and the wife see that she reverence her husband.

When Paul writes, "Submit yourselves one to another in the fear of God," he is speaking to husbands *and* wives. This places his next statement in context: **Wives submit yourselves unto your own husbands, as unto the Lord.**

Now there's a lot of kinky, wild, weird doctrines out there on submission. *Submission* literally means "to surrender your desires under the leadership of a godly husband."[1] Wives, if you and your husband are saved and filled with the Holy Ghost, then the call of God won't destroy your home.

Verse 25 says, **Husbands, love your wives, even as Christ also loved the church, and gave himself for it.** And how did Christ love the church? Through selfless sacrifice. Men, we have to be willing to sacrifice our very selves in order to develop the divine destiny of God in our homes. We need to sacrifice soulish, personal ambition that may go against the plan of God. It's a choice *we* make.

When God called me, I remember thinking to myself, *Well, okay, God, then I won't be a millionaire.* That wasn't easy for me, because I was a driven man. But I made a choice to say, "Okay, that's it. I'll back off. I don't want anything to do with making lots of money. I want the will of God. So Lord, I yield myself to Your will. I surrender myself to what You're saying and doing right now. Cindy and I submit to You in unity."

Never once has Cindy said, "No, we're not going to preach." Or, "We're not going to do this or that." Never once has she said, "Don't go and do what God has said." No, quite the contrary, she has always said, "What does the Lord say? What is the Spirit of God saying to you?"

I say, "Well, here's what I hear from God."

And her response is, "Amen. Let's do what God says."

Men, when you have a wife who stands in faith with you as you hear from God, there is nothing you desire that God will withhold from you. Thank God for godly wives who submit themselves to godly leadership! They're blessed! And thank God for men who love their wives and families as Jesus loved the church and gave Himself sacrificially for it.

the two highest callings

There are two high callings in life for all of us: (1) The high calling to serve God and fulfill the destiny of God and (2) the high calling to develop your family in Jesus Christ. Everything else in life is a distraction and must be prioritized under these two high callings, or it will cause you to miss the true call of God on your life.

Love your wife even as Christ loved the church. If your wife knows you would die for her, there's not much in this world she wouldn't do for you. When was the last time you looked her in the eye and said, "You know, *I would die for you* if I had to"? Wow! When was the last time you think she would have *believed* that statement?

4. *Develop conversations about what God is showing you*

If you're going to have a spiritual relationship, you need to be able to look your mate in the eye and say, "God said this to me." Or, "Last night I had a dream, and I know it was from God." (Not all dreams are from God, of course, but some are.) If you don't verbally share such spiritual experiences, your conversation will drift more and more toward carnal things, until the only things you ever talk about are the kids and what they did wrong.

One night I was in Mexico preaching at a revival meeting. About three o'clock in the morning, the Holy Ghost plainly spoke to me in a night vision regarding three different people in my church.

It was so powerful that I sat up in my bed; I knew it was God. I couldn't wait until daylight to call home. The first thing the next morning, I called Cindy and said, "Honey, I know that last night in a dream God said this to me. Go and find these three people and check on this situation. See what's going on."

So she went and checked on the situation, and it was exactly what God had shown me in the dream. Two of the three people were spared because the spiritual lines of communication in our marriage were open.

A home that has a powerful spiritual relationship develops "conference calls" with God. There must be more to conversation than what's on TV tonight. Learn to converse about what the Spirit of God is saying.

5. Be flexible

You must also be willing to change your mind about your spouse if you're going to have a spiritual relationship. Just about the time you *think* you have him or her figured out, something new may suddenly come up. Take a look at Joseph in Matthew 1:19:

Joseph her husband, being a just man, and not willing to make her a publick example, was minded to put her away privily.

Obviously, Joseph's heart was crushed, thinking Mary had had an affair. He was going to put her away privately because, by law, she could have been stoned for having a relationship with another man out of wedlock. On top of that was the embarrassment both of their families experienced. Joseph knew he couldn't marry his betrothed under these conditions. So Joseph, being a just and good man, made up his mind to put her away privately. Nobody would have known about it.

Now let's put ourselves in Joseph's place for a moment. This was a family with Jesus at the center of it. From the very beginning of their family life, Jesus was literally in the center. But even without the understanding of Mary's virgin birth, Joseph made up his mind and decided to protect her. "Okay," he said, "she's in sin, but I've made up my mind, and that's the way it is. I'm going to secretly put her away."

But then God began to interject His thoughts. Verse 20 says, **But while he thought on these things, behold, the angel of the Lord appeared unto him in a dream, saying, Joseph, thou son of David, fear not to take unto thee Mary thy wife: for that which is conceived in her is of the Holy Ghost.**

If you're going to have a spiritual relationship in your marriage, you must make a decision to have God's thoughts and allow them to change *your* thoughts.

Let me address husbands for a moment. Maybe you're planning a vacation to the Ozarks this year because you want to rent a rustic cabin and rough it. So you get your eleven fishing poles, two tons of tackle and two four-wheel drives up there. You're going up to the mountains to "get back to nature" so you can be close to God—and, of course, your better half. After all, you're going to be in "God's country."

But there's this other precious creature called your "wife" who hates having to clean the fish you'll catch over those two weeks. She also despises cooking fish on an open flame. And she certainly doesn't want to haul ten thousand pounds of moose meat ten miles over a mountain trail that's only been traveled on by badgers and armadillos!

Now, there's nothing wrong with a family vacation like that if *everybody* wants to do it. But sometimes a man will say, "I've made up my mind; that's where *I'm* going." And his little wife is over there saying, "Oh, God, please break his gun! Let someone steal the rods and reels, and don't let the police find them until after vacation!" She's in her prayer closet praying, because taking care of screaming kids who have never been to the mountains before, cleaning smelly fish and roughing it *is not* her idea of a *vacation!*

So she approaches her husband and says, "Honey, come, let us reason together. Though your sins be as scarlet, they will be white as snow!" (Isa. 1:18.)

But he's bound and determined, so he tells her, "I'm going to the mountains, and you are all coming—whether you like it or not!" Oh, is he in for a miserable two weeks!

The reality is that his wife needs a break, too. What seems like a vacation to him looks like two weeks of hard labor in a death camp to her—so he must learn to be flexible.

two little words

There are two little words you want to avoid using in marriage: "always" and "never." If you say to your mate, "Once I make up my mind, I never change it," you're going to be a miserable person for the rest of your life. Not only that, but you're going to make just about everybody around you miserable, too.

In order to have a spiritual relationship, you need to understand that God can interject thoughts into your mind that are different than your own. Your wife came from God, and she is to be overseen in a godly manner by her husband, not domineered with an iron fist.

Some people are so set in their ways that if someone disagrees with them, it goes against their grain to such an extent that it causes them to feel threatened. It's very difficult for God to use someone who has the same reply for every situation because he or she is inflexible. So again, *be flexible.*

This is important because you don't know everything. Every day you have the opportunity to learn something new, either naturally or spiritually. But if you refuse to change, you will short-circuit the godly relationship God wants you to have. Therefore, be willing to allow God to change your mind on things from time to time.

6. *Commit together to the move of God in the earth*

Last but not least among our marriage principles, couples need to commit as a team to the move of God in the earth. In Matthew 1:24, Joseph took Mary, committed to God's plan in their lives and took her to be his wife.

Then Joseph being raised from sleep did as the angel of the Lord had bidden him, and took unto him his wife [Mary].

If you're going to maintain a flowing and tender relationship, you must commit together as a husband and a wife to the move of God. Commit to pray and study the Word. That doesn't mean you have to necessarily sit side by side and read, but both of you must study the Word of God for yourselves.

Cindy has one spot where she likes to sit and read—a big, blue chair that used to be mine! She sits there and studies approximately two hours every night. I liked that chair, but that's her study place now. I either study on the couch, on the bed or in my little office. I'm kind of like a roving reporter, moving around the house until I can get comfortable. Although we sit in different places to study the Word of God, we're committed together to the move of God.

And here's a word concerning children. If they're ever going to see your commitment, you need to be faithful as a couple in attending the house of God. The highest form of love you can teach your children is to love the house of God and the leaders and the people in it. Train your children to love the glory and the presence of the Spirit of God.

The book of Acts refers to a couple whose names were Aquila and Priscilla. They took a young evangelist named Apollos into their home and explained the ways of Jesus to him. In the book of Romans, the apostle Paul wrote to the church at Rome and said, "Make sure you greet Aquila and Priscilla, the great teachers of the Word, who have done what was necessary to help infuse the gospel into that area." (Author's paraphrase. See Romans 16:3-4.) Aquila and Priscilla were a couple who were totally committed to the move of God.

As husband and wife, make a commitment to become involved in church activities. Sing in the choir together. "But I can't sing," you say. Well, then, make a joyful noise! Work in the nursery together sometime. Take tracts to do street witnessing. Work together in children's church, in an outreach ministry, in the TV ministry, or go visit a nursing home together. Commit together to the move of God in your family.

Once you've accomplished forming a spiritual relationship, you'll find the purpose and companionship in your home that is ordained through your covenant-keeping God.

a covenant marriage: anointed wine from God

The Bible is a book of relationships. The very theme of the Scriptures is God's plan to redeem mankind and restore the relationship with Him that we once had. Therefore, relationships are important to God, especially when a covenant is made.

But before a marriage covenant can be made between a man and a woman, they must first cut the apron strings.

leaving, cleaving and becoming one

The following verse out of Genesis 2 contains the great counseling session that God the Father, Jesus the Son and the Holy Ghost had in the Garden with the first husband and wife. God said they would "leave, cleave and be one."

> Therefore shall a man leave his father and his mother, and shall cleave unto his wife: and they shall be one flesh.
> Genesis 2:24

God says that leaving is necessary in His covenant of marriage. As a result, three things happen: A relationship is formed; fellowship takes place between the husband and wife; and a more intimate level of communication originates.

God clearly states that a man must leave his father and his mother. Not only that, but as God begins to draw a person to a mate, some relationships that person had as a single person may also need to be severed.

Your new marriage relationship will produce a fresh revelation of your relationship to Christ. Remember when you first came to Christ? The Holy Ghost began to sever some things in your former way of living. In the same way, when you find a godly husband or a godly wife, you start leaving some other things behind. Have you noticed that when God puts love in your heart for a man or a woman and that love begins to grow, there are some things of this world you want to leave? You may know fifteen other different men or women, but when God begins to put love in your heart for that "one-and-only," you begin to leave those superficial relationships behind.

Leaving and cleaving includes not only changing old relationships with your peers, but also with your own family of origin. A word of advice to newly married men: Never compare your wife's cooking with your mother's unless it's just as good or better. "Well, my mama cooks like nobody else. I should send you to live with Mama so she can teach you how to cook" is the wrong thing to say!

Now, I am very fortunate because my mother-in-law is Italian, and she can really cook. She trained my wife well before we were married, and I've had to diet occasionally because she is so good in the kitchen. But unfortunately not everyone can cook. Some men marry women who manage to even scorch water, and they tell their wives, "You can't cook worth a flip. I'm going to send you to live with my mother!" But they are only damaging their relationship by speaking down to her in such a way.

Some marriages' famous last words are: "My family didn't do it that way." You decrease the value of the relationship by comparing your marriage lifestyle with your parents' lifestyle. Constant comparisons such as those can violate the trust and confidence your husband or wife has in you. He or she will put up instant walls of defense. And unless a healing takes place by the Spirit of God, every time the subject is brought up for years to come, your spouse's defense mechanisms will kick in.

When you get married, be mature enough to leave the past behind and accept the man or woman God gave you—on his or her level. Men, God puts that responsibility mostly on *you*.

When God gave the command not to eat from the Tree of the Knowledge of Good and Evil, He was speaking to Adam. Then Eve was formed by God from one of Adam's ribs. Adam was given the responsibility of training his wife in the Word of God, but he didn't do it. Consequently, Eve usurped his role in the relationship, and that's when mankind fell.

How many homes since then have been destroyed because they're out of order? The first one got off track because God's order was not followed. Adam was to cleave unto his wife. That's what I call fellowship, because the word *cleave* in the Hebrew means "to cling, to hold on to or to fasten to."[1] He was to share all that God was to him with his wife. But he failed in his responsibility of leading his wife in the ways of God, and sin and heartache were the results.

leaving and cleaving is an act of the will

When God joins you and your mate together, He fastens you to each other. But marriage is an act of your will. The "bonds of holy matrimony" are an active choice that you make. It's not a feeling; it's a commitment. The first year or two of marriage may seem like paradise. But then the euphoria of being married will begin to wither away, and so may your emotional responsiveness to your spouse. Suddenly it doesn't seem as great as your first week of marriage. Don't attribute love to something you're doing or not doing, because all emotional experiences eventually wane. After being married fifteen or twenty years, sadly, some may not even care if their spouses come home at night. That's because they've forgotten how to cling.

God tells us to cling. We make the decision to be bonded to that particular man or woman, because in the course of life, differences come up that try to justify breaking our marriage bonds. Make a decision in your heart to be bonded to that man or woman whom God has given you.

About three years after Cindy and I were married, we weren't getting along very well, and I take the responsibility for that. The majority of it was my fault—I was very pigheaded. At that time I was in one of my "Hallam pity parties." We had bought a new home, and I was making good money.

Everything seemed to be going just the way we had planned. But then one day I was standing by a big, old pine tree in the backyard, and I began thinking, *She doesn't treat me right. She doesn't love me. I go out and work, beat my brains out bringing home the money. She can buy anything she wants. But she doesn't treat me right. She shouldn't talk to me like that.*

And then the Holy Ghost began speaking to me and said, "Do you see that pine tree there? What if I told you that for the rest of your life you were going to live under that pine tree? What would you do?"

I began thinking about it. *Well, I'd get a rake and get all that straw laid out just as I wanted it.* I thought, *Then I'd lay some boards and build them off that tree. I'd run lights from the house all the way down to the tree. And I'd get an outlet in there and have an air conditioner and a heater in that thing. I'd work on it every way I could to make it comfortable. I'd have the first pine tree condominium before it was over.*

Then the Spirit of God said, "What if I told you that you have to live with *her* for the rest of your life? I made you two as one, and as far as I'm concerned, you are to live with her forever. What are you going to do about it?" Let me tell you, when I heard that in my spirit, I immediately began to make some changes in my marriage!

If you allow Satan to enter your thought life, your mind will wander, and before long you'll find your actions are based on impulse. You will find yourself acting on emotions instead of making decisions based on the covenant you made with that person. It's the enemy's job to divide and conquer your family, but it doesn't have to happen. You can overcome those selfish thoughts and feelings of discouragement, and *you* can change.

In John 17, Jesus was in the Garden praying, "Father, I pray that they be one, even as we are one." God the Father and God the Son have different offices and different roles, but they have the same Spirit, the same unity, the same purpose, the same opinion and the same idea. God desires that husbands and wives should be one in the same way.

Men, as the leaders and priests in your homes (we'll discuss this later on), you need to pray that God will give you direction in your homes. And you need to pray that your wives will come into agreement with you. You don't need to walk in there and tell her, "Honey, we're moving to Kalamazoo, Michigan today. If you don't like it, just remember that I'm the man and you must submit to me!" Bad move. Wrong attitude. There she is with dreams of her own and looking for some sort of stability, when suddenly you say, "Hey, forget all that, we're going to do thus and such."

Brother, pray that God will give you wisdom so you can lead your home in such a way that your wife doesn't have any trouble getting into unity with you. Be willing to communicate, be vulnerable and develop godly character as a husband. If you communicate more effectively with your fellow employees than you do with your spouse, you've got a problem.

Even when you've had a hard day at work—remember that your spouse may have had a hard day, too. How many men come home and say, "Bring me a glass of tea while I watch the news"? Not even a "hello, Honey" or a "please"—they just come home and start barking orders. There's the man's wife—slaving over a hot stove all day or grappling with problems on the job all day, and all she wants is to have a nice conversation. But because you've talked all day long, you're ready to kick back and do nothing. And you will never develop as a husband or wife unless you're willing to practice communicating.

Satan will try to make communication with your husband or wife extremely distasteful for you. He will try to make you feel as if you're lowering yourself to talk to your spouse about something important in your day. But remember, unity will never come until you have communication.

Communication, as is everything in marriage, is an act of your will. You have to make a decision to deny your own preferences and begin to open up—and you start by communicating in small ways. If you're not a talker, then communicate by your actions. Reverse roles one week by coming home in the afternoon and vacuuming the house for her. What a word of communication that will speak! Come home and say, "Honey, I'm going to take you out for dinner tonight." You'd be surprised how that can open the door for great communication.

So make open communication an act of your will. Communication isn't a one-time experience; it has to be a way of life. Healthy communication between spouses will also develop godly character. You may say, "I'm just not a talkative person." But when you decide to talk to your husband or your wife, you develop as an individual through those interactions.

covenant purpose

A great philosopher once said, "Purpose is in the mind of the inventor." What a great thought! And it's true. So if you want to know the purpose for marriage, go back and find out what God, the inventor of marriage, was thinking when He created it.

Marriage is of God, and families come from God. And God's purpose for both of them is (1) to form a covenant, (2) to have companionship, (3) to bring forth children and (4) to have communion.

When a family is in unity, that unity releases power. When a family gets all of the working elements going in the same direction, they loose a dimension of power that can't be loosed any other way. First Peter 3:7 says:

> **Likewise, ye husbands, dwell with them according to knowledge, giving honour unto the wife, as unto the weaker vessel, and as being heirs together of the grace of life; that your prayers be not hindered.**

In other words, unity in marriage prevents prayers from becoming hindered. When God created the first family, He created it for the purpose of having companionship. Today, when a Spirit-filled husband and a Spirit-filled wife pray in unity according to God's purpose, things begin to happen. Remember, God's Word says, "One could chase a thousand and two could put ten thousand to flight." (Deut. 32:30.)

A covenant is a legal, binding contract, and every society, culture and religion recognizes marriage as a covenant. When a man and woman commit to one another, they enter into a covenant relationship. As Christians, our relationship is based upon the covenant made for us by God in Christ Jesus. We get married because God says it's time to get married, and we become equally yoked spiritually.

In the marriage covenant, a man establishes security that a woman can rely upon. When he leaves his mother and father, he walks away from their security. He doesn't leave his parents in the sense of not loving them or spending time with them. He leaves them because he is no longer dependent upon them. Some people get married and then they pull up to Mom and Dad's table with four kids and a wife and stay for months. And the husband wonders why he doesn't get any respect in that family!

Marriage means sacrificing your own desires for the sake of fulfilling your loved one's desires. The family is a place of sacrifice, but there's joy and satisfaction that comes from it. Just as God the Father sacrificed His only Son to save us, we need to learn to sacrifice for our families. We must learn in marriage how to deny selfishness by deciding that we are going to sacrifice—not each other, but *for* each other. We must also be willing to sacrifice for our children.

That's God's plan and purpose for your life. He will lead you through the stages of change. You didn't make a mistake when you entered into marriage. You may make mistakes because you neglect biblical principles. But that can change.

And if you want to know the right purpose for your relationship, go explore what the Manufacturer had in mind when He created it.

covenant companionship

Creating man and woman was in the mind of God from the foundation of the earth. And woman wasn't some afterthought that came when God discovered that Adam was lonely. He didn't say, "Well, I'd just better do something for Adam because he's out there working, and he's so depressed." No, God arranged it in His perfect timing. He spoke, creating man in His own image; "male and female He created them." (Gen. 1:27.) He spoke about making woman long before He finished His seven-day work. When He finished His seven days, He said, "Adam, now you get to work." Then in Genesis 2:18-25 we learn *how* He fulfilled Adam's need for covenant companionship when God said, "It's not good that Adam should be alone."

For Adam, the Bible says, **there was not found an help meet** (Gen. 2:20). There was not one found who would walk alongside him and help him fulfill the plan of God. So when that *one* was created to come *alongside* him, it was then that mankind could fulfill the plan of God in their lives.

My friend, that is exactly what you should desire in a husband or a wife. You should want someone who isn't just handsome or beautiful, but primarily someone who will help you obtain heaven in your home. You should want someone who will help you fulfill the plan of God—who will make up the "better half" of your "one flesh." When you have marriage covenant companionship, you have a covenant home.

A covenant home is a place where there is sharing in the Spirit. It is a place where everyone is going in the same direction in God—where you believe and speak in agreement. Even when you disagree, you don't worry in a covenant home, because you know that eventually you'll come to an agreement. It's a great place to be, because you're never afraid that some little disagreement will become a major falling out. When you happen to disagree about something, you can pray in the Spirit; then He will either correct your spouse, or He will correct you. And before it's over, you'll both be speaking the same thing.

Companionship is built around another word—*fellowship*. How can you have companionship without having some form of fellowship? Ephesians 5:23 says, **For the husband is the head of the wife....** But do you know what being the "head of the wife" actually means? It means direction. She's not looking for a boss or for someone to tell her what to do; she is looking for somebody to take the reins by taking the lead. Husband, your wife isn't looking for you to say, "Why don't you do this?" She's waiting for *you* to do that something first so she'll know how to follow your direction.

God put the man first for this reason—direction. The husband is in a home for protection, insight and direction. If you want divine fellowship, you must give direction by how you talk, commune and are willing to sacrifice. Verses 25 and

26 say, **Husbands, love your wives, even as Christ also loved the church, and gave himself for it; that he might sanctify and cleanse it with the washing of water by the word.** So God sanctifies and cleanses the church with the washing of water by the Word.

Your words are either cleansing and pure or stagnant and polluted. When you talk to your wife and to your children with understanding, you wash and cleanse your relationship with them by the water of your words. Speaking on a godly level doesn't mean you have to continually quote the Bible. Simply speaking with godly intent, purpose, integrity and encouragement will cleanse your family with the washing of water by your words.

covenant home

The first miracle Jesus performed during His earthly ministry took place at a marriage—the start of a covenant home.

And the third day there was a marriage in Cana of Galilee; and the mother of Jesus was there: And both Jesus was called, and his disciples, to the marriage. And when they wanted wine, the mother of Jesus saith unto him, They have no wine. Jesus saith unto her, Woman, what have I to do with thee? mine hour is not yet come. His mother saith unto the servants, Whatsoever he saith unto you, do it. And there were set there six waterpots of stone, after the manner of the purifying of the Jews, containing two or three

firkins apiece. Jesus saith unto them, Fill the waterpots with water. And they filled them up to the brim.
And he saith unto them, Draw out now, and bear
unto the governor of the feast. And they bare it. When
the ruler of the feast had tasted the water that was
made wine, and knew not whence it was: (but the
servants which drew the water knew;) the governor of
the feast called the bridegroom, And saith unto him,
Every man at the beginning doth set forth good wine;
and when men have well drunk, then that which is
worse: but thou hast kept the good wine until now.

John 2:1-10

In this miraculous account there were six empty waterpots—
empty and bone-dry. That's exactly how so many marriages
are—empty and bone-dry. But God intended for marriage to be
filled with love, joy and the anointing of the Spirit. Godly children, prosperity, good health, peace of mind and kind words
were all to be a part of it! So if you're going to have a covenant
family, understand that even though your marriage, or water-
pot, may seem dry right now, Jesus the miracle worker is on
hand to bring a change to the situation. A covenant marriage
and family should be a place of peace and rest. It is God's training ground for living in heaven one day.

the wine of God in marriage

I imagine the waterpots at that marriage feast were at first
full of dust and debris. Before the workers could fill the pots,

they had to rinse them out (washing of the water by the Word). Then they could be filled with the wine of God's blessings.

Realize the truth of this in your own life: Don't fill your life with problems. And don't marry someone who doesn't already have the wine of the Holy Ghost flowing through him or her powerfully in the courtship period.

I see six key elements in John 2:1-10 that I've entitled "The Wine of God in a Marriage." Let's take a look at them to see how they can help your marriage become all that God has destined it to be.

the wine of divine order

The first key is the wine of order. A family has a divine order to it, which the world doesn't understand. The world's order is the selfishness of men's, women's and now children's lib! This society of ours has fallen so far that a child can even sue his parents for divorce! How perverted and wretched people have become in their thinking! God didn't make the man to rule over the woman with an iron fist. No, He placed the man as the head, with the wife and children following respectively. God isn't a chauvinist—He simply created an order to protect and provide for women and children. And to see it operative, you must have the wine of His order of heaven in your home.

wine of self-control

The second wine poured out of a family is the wine of self-control. A family should be a family of self-control: not of impulsiveness or excessiveness; not of debt; not of immorality; but of self-control.

First Timothy 3 talks about how a bishop (leader) should live and rule his family with a spirit of self-control. So we ought to count the cost in advance, because a family should be *sober,* meaning "rational in thinking and reasoning."[2] Train your children to have self-control.

the wine of hospitality

The third wine is the wine of hospitality. Our homes should be filled with the dignity of graciousness. The Bible reminds us to be careful how we treat strangers, because many have entertained angels unaware. (Heb. 13:2.) Love other people and make them feel as if they're in their own homes when they come to visit. Even if you don't have the most beautiful china, a refrigerator full of food or designer linens, the most important thing is to make guests feel welcome and at ease. We do need to use wisdom concerning whom we let into our homes, especially for the sake of our children. But always remember that Jesus is a gracious Host—and follow His example.

the wine of enrichment

The fourth wine is the wine of enrichment. Spend quality time with your family. Don't just waste your precious time together in useless activities. Think of constructive ways to use time to impart to your family things that will increase, bless and enrich their lives.

When our children reached the age of five or six years old, we sent them to piano lessons. I didn't know if they were going to like it, but I knew that learning to play an instrument was a good way to enrich their lives. Our oldest daughter has especially enjoyed it, and all three of our daughters have won awards for their musical talents.

We also try to take two vacations a year—one is usually a fun trip, perhaps to an amusement park, and the other is educational, to a historic city or museum. One of the trips is what *they* like; the other is what *I* like.

the wine of enjoyment

The fifth wine is the wine of enjoyment. The Bible says in Proverbs 5:18, **Rejoice with the wife of thy youth.** Live joyfully with the wife of your youth. All work and no play makes Joe Schmoe a dull boy. I can hear it now: "I work seventy-five hours a week just to bring home the bacon for her." The problem is that she doesn't like bacon—she likes you! Little things mean a lot, and it may be something as simple as renting a romantic movie and sitting down together to watch it. You don't like that? Then take some time after a long day just to hold and cuddle your wife. Let her know that she is the most precious and valuable thing in your life. You'll be surprised how her whole demeanor will change.

Ladies, take at least one night a week to make your husband feel like a king. Use that time to enjoy a favorite hobby, sport or activity with him. Not many women really like stock car racing, football or wrestling, but make the effort to learn about what your particular husband likes. Learn to really enjoy sharing the experience with him because you love him, not necessarily because you love the activity.

And, both of you, don't lose the spontaneity you had when you were newly married. Maybe you say, "It's hard to be spontaneous when you've got kids running around the house." The fact that you now have children shouldn't be the downfall of enjoying one another. Teach your children to respect your time with your spouse, and don't be afraid when you guard your time that they will grow up to be insecure. It's really quite the contrary. When they see that you take time out to be with each other and love each other, they will feel more secure. Why? Because you've put your love for each other in action.

the wine of structure

The sixth wine is the wine of structure. Since you need time for your children and your spouse, you need to take time and sit down to eat a meal together. Our family tries to eat at least one meal together every day. Granted, that's not always easy when you're off to soccer, basketball and football games, gymnastics and piano lessons—but you'll find that having a meal together every now and then doesn't take a whole lot of effort. (Oh, and keep the TV off during meal times, too.)

Also structure your work time and work flow. Don't take every hour of overtime you can get just because of the money. Your family needs you more than the factory or the office does. If you have an opportunity to earn extra money, use wisdom. Don't take it just because it's available. Don't frustrate your family needlessly by being gone too much.

And ladies, before you run off to that big faith convention, see that the meals are cooked and the house is cleaned up. How many women rush out the door with overnight bags in hand, saying, "My favorite evangelist is in town, and I've got to go. So take care of the kids yourself. God's told me I need to go to this meeting, and I'm out of here!" Remember, God called you to be a wife and a mother first. Make sure you've taken care of the kids and your home first. There's nothing wrong with going to hear the Word of the Lord, but don't neglect your family in the process! Men, the same principle applies to you—don't neglect responsibilities as a husband and a father.

Here's one final important point of structure—designated bedtimes. When it's time to go to bed, it's time to go to bed. If you get your children in the habit of going to bed at a certain time it will be much easier for you to extend that time appropriately as they get older.

As God begins to fill your dry, empty waterpots full of the wine of His Spirit and a divine marriage relationship, His joy and peace will fill your family, and you will carry the anointed wine to pour out to others around you. With everyone pulling together, the support and covering of God—His mantle of grace—is extended over the home.

Chapter 3

God's mantle for the family

Anyone who builds a structure knows how important support is to that structure. If the support is missing or weak, or if it misses the mark by even a millimeter, the entire structure can collapse. So it is with the family. The support we receive from God as well as the support we receive from one another is vital to the stability of the home. In this chapter I want to take a close look at the structure of the family and how God designed it to stand strong in the face of trouble.

The Bible says, **And the Lord God caused a deep sleep to fall upon Adam, and he slept: and he took one of his ribs, and closed up the flesh instead thereof** (Gen. 2:21). Interestingly, the word *ribs* here is the same word for *beams*.[1] First Kings 7:2-3 uses the same definition of the word *beams* in reference to a "dove" beam. This type of beam requires you to dig several feet deep and wide and then pour concrete in the hole before you lower it. Solomon took particular beams, such as cedar beams, to support the temple he was building. He also used support beams to brace the ceiling of the temple.

So when the Bible says God took one of Adam's ribs, it's the same word in Hebrew as the word for a support beam that's standing upright. And it was for that kind of support that God created woman.

Your ribs protect vital organs such as your heart and your lungs. The ribs are an important support to your body.

Without them, you wouldn't be able to stand straight and upright. In the same way, a wife is a supporting part in the marriage relationship. The Bible says that Adam needed a help-mate—he needed a support. Maybe he got tired of naming all the animals and overseeing all of the works of God's hands completely by himself. So God looked at him and said, "You know, this guy needs some help!"

So God said, "I'll tell you what I'll do. I'll make him a helper, someone who will support him." Aren't you glad your wife is called to support you instead of just being some door-mat with no purpose or ambition? Isn't it wonderful that God is the original liberator of women?

In Solomon's building program, the support beam was to hold up a covering in the temple, and the Bible says that a husband is to be a covering to his wife. (See 1 Corinthians 11.) So a wife should support, and the husband should be a cover-ing as they complement one another in their roles.

Wives, you should be a tremendous support in your home. Don't tear your home down, and don't talk about how bad your husband is—pray for him. If he's an unbeliever, God says there's a way that you can convert him. If you'll support the relationship according to 1 Corinthians 7:12-16, and not give up on the Holy Spirit's power and influence through you, you'll eventually see the results. The Holy Ghost is bigger than your problem, and greater is He who's in *you* than he who's in your husband! Maybe you are saying, "You just don't know how bad he is." You're right; I don't. But I do know you're not called to take abuse, and I know the solution. The solution is

Jesus and being a support in your own home, never allowing yourself to tear the home down.

Husbands, you're called to be a covering in your home. Our society is trying to reverse the roles of males and females when they tell the woman she's just as good as a man. She is just as good, certainly, but the fact is she's not a man. Neither is a man a woman. So let's get the roles straight. The Bible and nature teach us that we're not the same. God never called a man to be a woman or a woman to be a man. He said a woman is a woman and a man is a man. One of them is a support, and the other is a covering.

In marriage, two become one, for they are bone of bone and flesh of flesh. In the eyes of God, everything about the two needs to go the same direction for the rest of their lives.

You say, "Well, I've got my own life to live." That's what American society and the world's humanistic society say. "You're your own person," they say. "Do your own thing." But that's a lie straight from the pit of hell, and it's Satan's way of dividing the family unit that God created. Marriage is not 50-50; it's 100-100 percent, with both partners giving it their all.

"my son, listen..."

When the woman fulfills her role as the support beam of the family and the man fulfills his role as the covering over the family, the children will take their places. There will come a time when you must let them go and believe by faith that the principles of God which you've taught them will remain with them for life. If you do your part while they're with you, I'm convinced it won't be too hard to let them go when the time comes. If they haven't had the principles of God instilled in them, they will be vulnerable to sin. You can't afford to just sit back and expect your family members to grow up by themselves. You must be an active participant in the role in which God has called you to walk.

People have a hard time letting go of their adult children when their own insecurities as parents surface because of guilt. They start thinking, *Dear God, what's going to happen to my kids now?* What they're really saying is, "I don't really trust God." Or, "I really didn't raise my children in the principles of God's Word."

Any time you see something in your children that is not of God, immediately discuss with them *why* it isn't of God—then hold fast to your decision. That's the only way you can instill principles in your children. You can't say, "Well, I told him that one time when he was seven years old. Now he's nineteen, and I just can't believe what he's doing." Maybe you told him one time, but since then he got infected with worldly "stinkin' thinkin'." So make a decision that when you discuss any principle, your *yea* will be *yea* and your *nay* will be *nay,* and do it with love.

Dad, you are a pattern, and unless something unusual takes place, your son will be a carbon copy of you when he gets married. Mom, you're a pattern, too. You are a walking visual aid to your daughter. I assure you that who you are in your home today, your daughter will be someday.

Do you remember how your mother used to tell you when you were growing up, "Someday when you have children, I hope you have seven just like you"? Do you remember your response? "I'll *never* treat my kids the way *you* treat me!" And now what do you do? You catch yourself all the time doing what you said you would never do.

Remember how your mother used to lick her thumb or spit on a tissue to wipe a little smudge mark off your face? Oh, how you swore you'd never humiliate your children like that. Now what do you do? You unconsciously do the same thing as you watch your child roll his eyes. Why? Because you are a duplicate of what you saw in your home as a child.

So if you don't like something about your life, then get rid of it! Your child will grow up and duplicate that very same thing one day unless the Holy Ghost intervenes.

Another aspect of the covering of the family is discipline. Solomon spoke these words in Proverbs 5:1-2:

> **My son, attend unto my wisdom, and bow thine ear to my understanding: That thou mayest regard discretion, and that thy lips may keep knowledge.**

Solomon's parents, King David and Bathsheba, gave him this valuable advice. David was a great warrior on the battlefield, but his strategy on the home front was the pits. He and some of his other wives had sons who were real rascals. One of his sons, Amnon, raped his half-sister, Tamar. Another son, Absalom, tried to overthrow David for the throne and killed his half-brother, Amnon. David had all kinds of problems with his kids because he probably never said NO to them about anything.

Stare into those big blue eyes or those big brown eyes and determine to say no sometimes. Otherwise, your children will grow up thinking things in life will always go their way. When they're old enough to compete in the world and someone tells them no, they'll do what they want to do anyway. They will never develop character, learn to accept responsibility or handle difficult situations, because they never will have had to deal with them.

In the Hebrew, a son is a builder of the family name. So David was speaking to the one to whom he was going to pass his mantle. David was saying, "Solomon, Son, I want you to listen to me now—I want you to hear what I'm saying, because there's going to come a time when you'll have to make decisions that discriminate between good and evil. Walk in knowledge instead of walking in ignorance. Listen to what I say!"

Take time to sit down and talk with your children. Believe that the Word of God you have instilled in them will be wisdom to them, because you can't be with them twenty-four hours a day. It's not the public school system's job to teach wisdom to your children. They may give them some knowledge, but wisdom comes from God. Besides, for the most part, our public school system today totally defies the name of God. So you are sadly mistaken if you're expecting teachers to impart wisdom, morality or discrimination between right and wrong to your kids. Before you know it, your children come home with a totally different philosophy ingrained in them than what you might have thought.

Sit down with your children today and say, "This is not right, and this is why it is not right. We are Christians, and this is what God says about it!" Tell them what happens—what the consequences are—when they act like the world. Also tell them what happens when they act like Jesus. Be blunt sometimes—not hard, but blunt. Be honest, because you can be sure that what's being taught to your children outside of your godly home is not only blunt—it's also ungodly.

In Proverbs 6:20, David told Solomon, **My son, keep thy father's commandment, and forsake not the law of thy mother.** In other words, he said, "Now listen to me, Solomon, and don't forget what your mom said to you also." So, Mom, your part in helping build a family is just as important as Dad's.

Mothers, one of the most dangerous things you can say to your son or daughter is "Just wait until your daddy gets home—he's going to get you." Why? Because a child hearing those words will grow up respecting daddy, but he will run all over you. When both of you make a rule, you see to it yourself that they do it.

You say, "But it's so much easier if I let their father handle it. I'm so tired of having to lay down the law." Okay, but the problem is you don't know what tired is until that child turns sixteen or seventeen and he's in trouble. You don't know what a sleepless night is until you can't sleep four nights in a row because you're trying to get him out of jail. So if you do your part today, you won't have to worry about it tomorrow.

Here's another great piece of advice: Watch out for flattering words. **For the lips of a strange woman drop as an honeycomb, and her mouth is smoother than oil: But her end is bitter as wormwood, sharp as a twoedged sword** (Prov. 5:3,4). The word *wormwood* means "a poisonous drug."[2] Wormwood was used to create a drug much like our narcotics today. Verse 4 says, "Her end is as bitter as a drug addict's, and her words are as sharp as a double-edged sword."

Flattery is one way people will try to gain your trust in order to take something from you. Watch out for people who are always flattering you, because it won't be long before they're going to want something from you. A compliment, on the other hand, always adds to you. People who give genuine compliments seek to encourage you.

So parents, train your children to use wisdom. Husbands and wives, just because someone of the opposite sex comes to you and begins to flatter you doesn't mean you have to receive what they are saying.

I personally don't like women coming up and flattering me—not that anybody would ever want to—but I don't like it. You say, "Oh, that's because you're an old prude." No, that's because the Word of God says I have wisdom when I avoid those kinds of situations. I've decided there is just one woman in this world for me.

When you live purely yourself, it is easier to train your children to live purely as well. Make the decision to raise your children according to the principles of God. ...**Among the simple ones, I discerned among the youths, a young man void of understanding, Passing through the street near her corner; and he went the way to her house** (Prov. 7:7,8). Another word for *passing* is sauntering. To *saunter* is to "wander around aimlessly as if you're bored and without a purpose."[3]

Keep your children occupied with activities. When they're old enough, teach them how to make their own beds and pick their own clothes up off the floor. Sometimes that's easier said than done, but it can be accomplished. Teach the Word of God to them with love. Don't force feed it to them. Just be consistent with the Word of God and inspire them with the things of God. The Bible says we should meditate on the things of God and that we have the choice of casting down any negative thought pattern that tries to penetrate our lives. We need to think, choose and act wisely—to the point that it becomes the standard for our lives. When the Word of God is active in our lives, we become more sensitive to the voice of the Holy Spirit.

It's up to you to learn His Word. So soak yourself in the presence of the Holy Spirit, and you will know His plan for your family. Cover yourself with the mantle of God's covenant—His Word—and cloak your family with prayer. Husbands lead, wives support and children imitate what they see in their parents. When you build God's way, He will be the foundation, and everyone living under His covering will rest in His strength.

Part II

Men Are Tupperware, Women Are China

superglue for
your relationship

"What God has joined together, let no man put asunder." This traditional wedding pronouncement is where most wedding ceremonies end and most marriages begin. Unfortunately, the spirit of this world doesn't support unity, and "'til death do us part" is now "'til I-get-sick-and-tired-of-this-marriage do us part."

We have become a throw-away society in which the value of life is cheap. People are quick to save the whales, but they murder and throw away thousands of unborn babies every day. And that cheap mentality of murderous convenience has become more prevalent among marriages today. If we don't like what our spouses are doing, we get rid of them. Some people are even under the impression that their new life in Christ means getting rid of their unsaved spouses. But that's not so, because God's Word is clear that marriage is for life.

> Some Pharisees came and tested him by asking, "Is it lawful for a man to divorce his wife?"
>
> "What did Moses command you?" he replied.
>
> They said, "Moses permitted a man to write a certificate of divorce and send her away."

"It was because your hearts were hard that Moses wrote you this law," Jesus replied. "But at the beginning of creation God 'made them male and female.' 'For this reason a man will leave his father and mother and be united to his wife, and the two will become one flesh.' So they are no longer two, but one. Therefore what God has joined together, let not man separate.

Mark 10:2-9 NIV

Most people see the wedding vows they made as promises to one another. But a covenant is more than a promise. Most newlyweds even think the word *vow* means promise. But a vow and a promise are two different things. A promise is based upon your ability to commit, whereas a vow (or a covenant) is based upon a resolve to be committed regardless of the circumstances. That is what happened when you married, and that is the plan of God, the Author of marriage.

"Well, I didn't know what I was getting into," you say. I've got news for you—you did, but you chose to ignore the truth.

Have you ever signed a promissory note without knowing what you were signing? Try explaining to the bank that you didn't know a certain clause was in there. In so many words, they'll tell you, "Tough luck, Charlie." Marriage is the same way, only it's not ordained by mere human law. It is ordained in heaven. Marriage is more than just "living together" or giving each other a series of promises we can make and break at will. It's a covenant. God is the witness to the covenant, and He intends for your marriage relationship to last "until death do you part."

the hardness of men's hearts

Opposites attract, so often the very traits that attracted us to our spouses at first, repulse us after marriage. Little by little, that one annoying habit grows until we've made a mountain out of a molehill. We become hardhearted, and we decide to separate because of "irreconcilable differences." Divorce isn't a twentieth century problem. It existed during Jesus' time—and even in the days of Moses.

> Pharisees also came unto him, tempting him, and saying unto him, Is it lawful for a man to put away his wife for every cause? And he answered and said unto them, Have ye not read, that he which made them at the beginning made them male and female, And said, For this cause shall a man leave father and mother, and shall cleave to his wife: and they twain shall be one flesh? Wherefore they are no more twain, but one flesh. What therefore God hath joined together, let not man put asunder. They say unto him, Why did Moses then command to give a writing of divorcement, and to put her away? He saith unto them, Moses because of the hardness of your hearts suffered you to put away your wives: but from the beginning it was not so.
>
> Matthew 19:3-8

It was because of the hardness of men's hearts that Moses allowed them to divorce their wives. But Jesus said, "From the beginning that was not God's plan." And it's still not God's plan. The reason why people divorce, bottom line, is because one partner—if not both—becomes so hardhearted that he or she simply won't bend enough to meet the other person halfway. The bitterness and hurt build up for years until people become so callous that there's no hope for them in the natural. Only God can take a heart of stone and replace it with a heart of flesh.

Wives, perhaps your husband isn't serving God. Still he is in a godly position as the husband, which in God's order of creation is the first place in the home. So if you want to keep your home together, learn to have a quiet and meek spirit. Don't backbite, even when your husband messes up. I promise you, he will mess up sometimes, because he's not perfect.

God's divine order

Role reversal is another way the devil has tried to destroy marriages. Many women domineer their families because men allow them to. But when the role of each partner is out of order, chaos is the result.

God has called the man to be the head of the home. And as I've explained, leading isn't dominating. If the woman is trying to rule the home, then that home is out of order. If the man is not serving God and leading his household in God's plan, then he is out of order in his own home. That's one reason why there are so many problems. Some men say, "I've learned how to get out of that problem—I just throw my hands up and let my family do what they want to do." But let me tell you, it won't work; and you will never be satisfied, nor will your mate. There's order in everything God does.

Sir, when you get married, be willing to apply the Word and give yourself for your wife. Ephesians 5:25,28 says, **Husbands, love your wives, even as Christ also loved the church, and gave himself for it.... So ought men to love their wives as their own bodies. He that loveth his wife loveth himself.** The Bible says to love your wife as if she were an extension of your own flesh. Your wife is not just some woman you wake up next to every morning—she is an extension of your own flesh.

Did you ever hit your finger with a hammer and feel a sharp, throbbing pain? I'm sure you didn't say, "You stupid finger. I can't believe you're hurting like that!" No, the first thing you do when your thumb gets hit with a hammer is to grab it. "Oooh! It hurts. Quick, put some ice water on it! Get a Band-Aid, get me to the doctor, put me out of my misery—anything, but do something! Help!" That's a typical knee-jerk reaction when your flesh is hurting and in pain.

When your wife hurts, you should hurt too because she is an extension of your flesh. You don't need to run her off because she's hurting. You need to hold her and say, "What's the problem? What can I do to help? Where does it hurt?" As her husband, you are called to love her as your own flesh.

Ephesians 5:22 says, **Wives, submit yourselves unto your own husbands, as unto the Lord.** "To him?" you wives may ask. "My own husband? That guy I live with? Me, submit myself to him?" That's right, because inside every wife is an intense desire to please her husband. God said it was so from the beginning when He told Eve that her desire would be for her husband. (See Genesis 3:16.)

Even Sarah obeyed Abraham, calling him *lord*, which means "my head."[1] Notice it's with a lowercase "l," not a capital "L." There can only be one Lord. And also notice that she didn't call him names such as, "Hey, you jerk," "Hey, you bum," or "Hey, you adulterer, trying to give me away to some old king." Although Abraham had done such foolish things, she still had a godly reverence for him and a meek spirit. Sarah didn't surrender her will to his sin, but neither did she usurp his authority as the head of the home. Instead, she let Abraham be Abraham and God be God—knowing that all would end well.

Although it is God's will for you to be in submission to your husband, God doesn't say to stay and take abuse of any kind. If you're fearful for your life—fearful of being beaten, fearful of being killed—then GET OUT. God has *not* called you to be anybody's punching bag; He's called you to be a child of the King. And you can't joyfully serve your husband to draw him back to the love of the Lord when you're constantly in fear and being violently abused.

"stick-to-it-iveness"

Many men live with their wives, treating them as men instead of women. They mentally, physically, verbally and emotionally treat their wives like men 99 percent of the time.

Then when such a man wants to arouse his wife he suddenly wants her to be a woman. When she doesn't respond, the husband may try to use force, manipulation or control. You cannot treat your wife the way you do another man and then expect her to respond to you as a woman!

When the Bible says that a man should leave his father and mother and cleave to his wife, the word *cleave* in the Hebrew means "to stick to like a glue."[2] And that is the only way a couple can become complete, according to God.

To *cleave* is "to glue yourself to each other." Literally the two become one flesh, a single unit instead of two ambitions living under one roof. Matthew 19:6 says, **Wherefore, they are no more twain, but one flesh. What therefore God hath jointed together, let not man put asunder.** The word *joined* is another tense of the word *cleave*. It is a stronger form of the word *cleave*. It's like the difference between normal glue and superglue. Superglue doesn't break down and come unglued as easily as normal glue. So to cleave in marriage is like literally being superglued to each other. That's the type of "stick-to-it-iveness" a marriage should have so that when the storms of life blow, the marriage remains intact.

the heartbreak of divorce

I once glued two pieces of wood together with epoxy glue. Then I thought, *Well, that's not where that's supposed to go, so I'll break it apart and reposition it.* But little did I know that it had become bonded together. When I tried to separate it, I tore part of the wood off.

In the same manner, when a man and a woman get married, they don't just start living together. They enter into a divine state created in heaven. This is why whenever there's a separation or divorce, people feel as though their hearts are being torn apart. There is literally a tearing apart of two souls that had been one.

There's no such thing as a *peaceable* separation. You may have a peaceable separation over material possessions, but your emotions, hearts, minds and, yes, even your children will splinter and break. It's the death of a marriage, and the casualties and damages are irreparable.

The hardening of hearts is the reason that divorce exists. When the heart of one person—male or female—becomes hardened toward the other mate, it's a tearing, difficult time. It's the height of rejection, hurt, insecurity and fear.

Men say, "It's not may fault. It's her fault." Women shift the blame right back and say, "Well, it's not my fault—it's his fault." But the truth of the matter is they both have hard hearts, and only Jesus can heal hearts. Ezekiel 36:26 NIV says, **"I will give you a new heart and put a new spirit in you; I will remove from you your heart of stone and give you a heart of flesh."** Now that's good news! God can heal both your spouse and you, even if you believe there is no hope.

Perhaps you're reading this book and you've gone through a bitter divorce and a custody battle. It is very important to recognize that your past is your past. You can't unscramble eggs, so don't try to figure out what you could have done and didn't do. Thank God from this point that you can rise up and live according to the Word of God. God will forgive you of your past if you repent. It's not *you* that God is displeased with, it's the sin you have committed. But if you have repented, your sins have been removed from you as far as the east is from the west.

For too long the church has condemned divorcees and, at times, treated them as spiritual lepers. If God doesn't condemn you, my friend, then you are free. Learn what God wants to teach you, and then move on. Allow His healing balm to soothe your wounded soul. He specializes in picking up the pieces and putting them back together again.

bonded together, forever

Everyone wants unity, but it doesn't come automatically; there is a pathway to unity. It begins with communication that prioritizes in a marriage what's out of order with the Word of God.

Speak this confession in your life: "From now on, my relationship will not be a demanding one but will be one of communication. I'm married to a helpmate, not a slave, so I will communicate what we can do together instead of always demanding my own way. I'll demonstrate my words by my actions as to what should be done in the house. I won't chastise my mate simply for leaving something undone because I failed to communicate my wishes."

Communication and fellowship produce unity in the relationship. If you are married and not in unity of purpose or mind, make a decision together to begin communicating. If you learn to communicate with one another, you will eventually fellowship together. It's a wonderful, beautiful experience when a husband and wife have fellowship. The more you fellowship, the stronger your relationship grows, which brings about unity.

You become like-minded with your spouse when you pray for him or her. Suddenly, when you sit down to discuss the bills, you don't ring the bell for that once-a-month fight. Instead, you sit down and have one mind on how you're going to dispense that money. If you've prayed over the matter, it's incredible how peace inundates your whole being.

Few men ever give of themselves entirely to their wives. They have their own priorities in life—their jobs, their egos, their own desires and their own paychecks. But men, in order to give of yourself to your wife, you have to change your priorities. Before marriage, your priorities were in this order: me, myself and I. Everything you did revolved around your own world. If you wanted to do it, you did it. You were a single, carefree man, and nobody got in your way to keep you from doing whatever you wanted. "If I want to do it, I just get in the car and go. If I get fired from my job, I'll just get another one." Remember that?

But it's not that simple when you're married, because when you get fired, she gets fired. You're not working for yourself; you're working for her first, then for those precious children God gave you. The family that doesn't have Jesus as its centerpiece doesn't have any glue to hold it together when the storms of life blow.

So believe God for a spirit of unity. Actively pursue the spirit of unity and a bond of peace in your marriage. The Bible says if you have peace, it will bond you together. Men and women who are not at peace with themselves will not be at peace within a local church or in their relationship with God. When you see people who are nervous, erratic and not faithful to the house of God, many times it's because there is no bond existing in their marriages.

The absence of sin and rebellion creates a bond to the body of Christ. (See Ephesians 4.) And I don't know about you, but there are two things I want to be bonded to in this life: my wife and the body of Christ. When you don't sinfully mistreat your mate, you can be bonded to each other. When you don't have sin between you and God, you have a bond to the body of Christ. Then you can dwell in peace with the wife of your youth, bonded in unity, truly together forever.

tupperware versus china

How often have you heard men say, "I'll just never understand women"? That's because most men haven't grasped the fact that women are created differently. As I've said, many times men treat women like they would other men. Likewise, some women treat men like they are women. Then misunderstandings occur, and we walk away from each other saying, "I just don't understand that person. It makes sense to me, and yet it makes no sense to him (or her) whatsoever." The problem is in how men and women have been created—fundamentally different.

The difference between fine china and Tupperware is that even though both hold the same amount (if they're equal in size), one of them is a finer vessel. And to me the problems of male/female misunderstanding can be dealt with through this simple illustration. Fine china is very fragile, but Tupperware is tough and coarse. Men are like Tupperware, and women are like fine china. Both a china cup and a Tupperware cup can hold a cup of coffee. But men, like Tupperware, can take many more bumps along the way, and women, like china, need to be handled with care. God didn't say that men are superior to women. Women can count, think, talk, reason and do everything else just as well as men can—often better. What God did say is that she is a finer, or a weaker, vessel. And the problem today is that many men are dropping their "china dolls."

Peter says a man should dwell with his wife according to knowledge.

> Likewise, ye husbands, dwell with them according to knowledge, giving honour unto the wife as unto the weaker vessel, and as being heirs together of the grace of life; that your prayers be not hindered.
>
> 1 Peter 3:7

"he says, she says"

Men tend to think logically about things, and women tend to think emotionally. For instance, I remember when Cindy and I first got married, I sold my Chevy Vega, got a good job and purchased a Pontiac Grand LeMans. I had just left the Air Force, and I really wanted this car! It was the finest maroon-colored Grand LeMans ever made, with a 400XY super-charged engine, dual glass packs, dual exhausts, a white vinyl top, white interior and black carpet. Brother, it was hot—and it purred like a kitten! No one could touch that car in my hometown. I'd get out there and wax and polish it until the sun's reflection bouncing off every inch of its gleaming body blinded me.

I'll never forget the day I drove the car home, and Cindy said, "I want another car." Man, I just knew the honeymoon was over!

"You what? You want another car? This is the fastest, hottest running car on the planet. This car is beautiful. It has a white interior; it's got a powerful engine. Why?" I asked.

"I don't like the way it sounds," she replied.

So, I got another car! Why? Because it wasn't *my* car only. It was *our* car, and the hot rod boom under the hood embarrassed the other owner.

Another difference between the genders is that men tend to come across rather indifferent and impersonal about things, whereas women tend to take things more personally.

For instance, I watch the news at night to stay current with what's going on in the world. If the news reporter states, "Bombing and shooting occurred in Israel today. There were also typhoons, earthquakes and floods in the Far East, causing total devastation," I sit there thinking, *Hurry up and get to something else. I've heard that already.* But my wife tends to personally identify with the information she hears until it begins to have an effect upon her.

So, men, if you don't understand what makes women tick, you won't understand their responses. And ladies, when a man zones out, it doesn't necessarily mean he's mean and insensitive. It simply comes with the male package. We're just not as emotionally involved with things that don't personally affect us.

Men also tend to be very goal-oriented in life, whereas women tend to be more relationship-oriented. Men are success-oriented while women are security-minded. He says, "I'm going to take everything out of the savings account and invest it in this business plan. It's all or nothing, Babe. What do you say?"

"You pull one penny out of there, and you're dead meat," she replies!

The maternal instinct kicks in. They've watched you blow your money for years, so they want to make sure there's enough money to feed the kids next week. It's a package deal, men. And if you get rid of the lady you have now, the next one will be just like her. They're not the ones with the problem; you are, if you don't understand what makes them tick.

Females tend to need roots—they need a house, a place to call their own. They need a place where they can feel secure, and they like it kept a certain way. They have a measure of security in the way things are kept.

Whenever guests offer to help clean up the kitchen, women usually say, "No, thank you. I appreciate your offering to help, but you sit down and make yourself comfortable." She's being a gracious hostess, but what she's really saying is, "If I let this person help me, it's going to take me three days to try to find the dishes."

Men just walk into the house "as is." And some ladies have to literally house train their husbands. Some insensitive clods walk in with grease or mud on the bottom of their shoes and track it all over the carpet. Forget the fact that you have to steam clean carpets these days. Then they look back and say, "I didn't do that. My shoes did it." Just because he's a soup brain, ladies, doesn't mean it's time to get a divorce. It's simply time to understand there are some basic differences.

prophet, priest and king

When you discover who Jesus is, you discover who you should be in your home, but many men don't want to live like Christ. They don't want to love their families like Christ does.

They want to do their own thing, be their own man, come in and sleep, eat, drink, get up and leave and turn in a paycheck once a week.

God said, "I will never leave you; I will never forsake you. I will be with you always." (Deut. 31:6.) Sir, if you haven't absorbed that mentality yet, then you need to begin to renew your mind regarding family relationships. Much of your wife's strength is drawn from you. Much of your children's stability—mentally, socially and financially—comes from you. When men don't fulfill their rightful roles, children often grow up rebellious, insecure and emotionally fragile.

Contrary to popular belief, you aren't called to be a *boss* in your home. You are called to be a *priest* in your home. You may say, "I'm the boss of my house, and a man's home is his castle." Man, are you setting yourself up for a fall! Hey! Get it straight. You're not the boss in your house, men. You are representing Christ in your home. Christ led by serving, not demanding— and there is a difference. You are a prophet, priest and king.

You should be the instigator of love in your home in your words and in your deeds. If you're married and don't understand that, then you're trying to make it work using the wrong set of instructions.

marriage comes with a set of instructions

We have a home computer that came with all the bells and whistles. I'm not really computer savvy yet, and one day I really messed the thing up.

I was playing the only thing I know how to play on it—golf! Just as I was about to shoot par, all of a sudden that computer died on me, and I couldn't get that golf game to come back up. Now, I don't know how to fix a computer, but I got in there and acted like an IBM repairman. I turned every switch off and on. Then I punched the enter key, the delete key, the escape key—I punched all the keys. I started punching buttons I didn't even know were there! I thought, *Well bless God, if it blows up, I'll be no worse off.*

Finally, this brother came over to the house, and he started doing things by the instruction manual. A click here and a click there, and in three minutes he had it running again. The next thing I knew, up came the golf game on the screen, and Arnold Palmer and I started down the fairway again.

That's a good example of what happens with married couples. They get married, but they don't use the instruction manual. So they start trying to blindly fix it with their own ideas of what might work, and they only make things worse. Your marriage is from heaven. It's not carnal—it's supernatural. If you start tinkering with your marriage without the proper instructions, just as would happen with a computer, you're going to mess things up.

You have to play the game by the rules in order for it to work. And the first rule is this: *Husbands, love your wife as Christ loved the church.* After Jesus, your wife must be the number one priority in your life. If your wife is successful, you will be successful as a man. If she's happy, emotionally stable and loves to be around you, then you will be fulfilled. If you look her in the eyes and talk to her, and she talks back to you in a gentle manner, you are a success—and your home is a success.

Wives, don't run yourselves down. Don't go around saying you're no good, you're not pretty or you're too fat. You don't need to tell your husband how ugly you think you are, because you are the crown of *his* life. Some ladies feel bad about themselves, so they look in the mirror and feel ugly, old and fat. They notice how many wrinkles they have, how many gray hairs they have, and they begin to tell that to their husbands.

"I'm getting so old I can't do anything anymore. I'm just so old; I feel like a grandma."

"Well, how old are you?" he asks.

"I'm thirty-two," she says.

Yep. You're ancient. Give me a break! Life's just getting started.

Understand that God says you are literally an extension of your husband's life. So when you sit around running yourself down, you're running him down. That's why it's good to fix yourself up and take care of yourself. As we say in Texas, "Every barn needs a little paint!"

Husbands and wives, learn to ask why your mate is hurting. Remember, hurts are emotional, and they have a long-running effect. Don't say, "I don't understand that woman. Every time I turn around, she's crying over something. I don't understand."

I once heard about a guy who was watching a football game on television. His wife was in the kitchen slicing vegetables when she cut her finger and started hollering, "Oh my!

Oh my! I'm hurt! I'm hurt!" And the guy just sat there, watching television. She was screaming "Oh, my finger is cut. I cut my finger!" Finally the guy snapped out of it, ran to her and said, "Dear God, I thought I was going deaf." That's the way some husbands listen to their wives, but it doesn't have to be that way.

Bitter and sweet water can't flow out of the same vessel, but Tupperware and china *can* compliment one another. Make a decision to be kind and tenderhearted to one another. The Bible tells us to "be tenderhearted." (See Ephesians 4:32.) Find out why she's hurting or why he's upset. Remember, men, your wife is fashioned out of finer material. Don't just say, "Bless God, every time she gets mad, I tell you what happens. We're just going to have a war." Don't say that—instead ask yourself, *What is stressing my fine piece of china?*

If you'll find out why your spouse is hurting in a certain area, it's incredible how that will release and heal him or her. Just the fact that you are compassionate toward that hurt will minister tremendously.

The highest priority in your life after your relationship with God should be making your household a place of love and peace—tupperware and china reflecting God's best, holding, doing what God fashioned them to do.

Learn to forgive one another by being able to see your *own* faults. If you can see your own faults and weaknesses, you will never have trouble forgiving your spouse. As long as you are trying to prove you're right, however, you can't be a person of forgiveness.

When was the last time you told your spouse, "I'm sorry," or, "You know, you're right; I was wrong"? Your spouse's jaw would probably drop if he or she heard those words from your mouth!

Part of ministering grace to your spouse is through edifying communication. Ephesians 5:4 warns about filthiness, foolish talking and jesting. Foolish jesting is insensitive joking. For instance, men, don't pick on her about her weight when you know it hurts her. Ladies, don't joke about his receding hairline when he really can't do anything about it. Support him and love him. Don't run down your mother-in-law when you know it causes a problem. There are areas people joke about that in actuality hurt deeply. Although it may be a big joke to you, when all is said and done, another wound can be opened—and the scar will remain. And men, when you stomp around your home like a bull in a china shop, you wonder why she breaks out in tears. It's because you've smashed her to pieces. You've inflicted one hurt on top of another.

for husbands- and brides-to-be

One of the great benefits of being married to a Spirit-filled person who walks uprightly and lives according to the Word is that you don't have to be lonely. Life is long, and although it has a lot of good times in it, it has some bad times too. But when you have the right spouse, you can overcome the tough times and avoid loneliness in the process.

For those of you who are single and desire to be married, make your priority to do what God calls you to do. Serve

God and He will bring you that person who is best suited for your needs in *His* time. Don't go out, try a few and discard the ones who aren't compatible. All you'll do is lose a part of yourself every time.

According to the plan of God, marriage completes a man and a woman, and it completes the plan God has for your lives. So learn to serve. In the process of serving and obeying God, rest, knowing that He will give you a Spirit-filled husband or wife. God will bring that man or woman to you—it's just a matter of time.

Every day you should make a decision to pray. Praying should come as naturally to you as breathing. Then when God brings that person into your life, your family altar time will be natural. Paul tells us in Romans 8 that God doesn't condemn us, because Jesus is interceding for us. As I was reading that one day, the Holy Ghost said to me, "Anything that you pray over, you won't condemn." If you will pray over your wife every day, you will not condemn her or treat her unfairly.

And remember, men, in Ephesians 5:20-21, the apostle Paul says that husbands and wives should submit themselves to one another in the fear of the Lord. Many people are hooked on this submission doctrine, and they take it out of context to the point that it's almost a cultish thing. Get that straight now.

God wrote specifically to the wife *and* to the husband and said, "Submit to one another." So forget this fleshly macho thing that says, "Me Tarzan, you Jane!" and demands that the wife submit. It's guaranteed you're going to have trouble in your relationship and every other area if you've got that pathetic attitude that only covers your own inferiority.

dealing with her in harmony

Men, any time you tell your wife, "God said for you to submit to me," you have totally distorted the Word of God. That's something between her and God, and it comes with the role she's been placed in. She has the privilege of humbling herself in the ministry of a wife, just as much as you are called to submit and humble yourself unto her as your wife.

If you say, "I'm not humbling myself to any woman," then the odds are that you'll have to go through a world of heartache until you find someone emotionally crippled enough to put up with your foolishness. And really, why would you even want that?

God never told you to manipulate your wife. He will never tell you to force your wife to do anything. He says, "As a male, you are placed in the role of a husband." But one of the greatest tragedies today in many marriages is that men don't truly know their wives.

Men are naturally stimulated by sight. Women are stimulated, most of the time, by emotions. A man may fantasize in his mind about how he would like his wife to be. His wish list may be developed through magazines, TV or film. When she doesn't live up to those expectations, suddenly there's friction in the home. She can't become what she is not. And there is nowhere in Scripture that directs men to have preconceived ideas about their wives' traits and physical characteristics. The Bible says men should know their wives and dwell with them according to knowledge. (See 1 Peter 3:7.) Husbands, God didn't command you to dwell with your spouse according to lust. He said, "Dwell according to knowledge." Know her as an individual. Her emotions need to be taken care of and honored, men. So dwell with your wife according to godly knowledge, not according to manipulation, force or demand.

When you dwell with your wife according to God's divine plan and give honor unto her as the finer, or weaker, vessel, you will experience the peace that comes as co-heirs of the grace of life. The grace of life is everything that God has offered you through Jesus Christ.

women: the finer things in life

> Whoso findeth a wife findeth a good thing, and obtaineth favour of the Lord.
>
> **Proverbs 18:22**

Very often men are successful and achieve a favorable status in life because of the women they marry. God grants men favor because of the women they travel the road of life with. It's written in the Word. The Bible refers to those ladies as "virtuous women."

a priceless treasure

Who can find a virtuous woman? for her price is far above rubies. The heart of her husband doth safely trust in her, so that he shall have no need of spoil. She will do him good and not evil all the days of her life. She seeketh wool, and flax, and worketh willingly with her hands. She is like the merchants' ships; she bringeth her food from afar. She riseth also while it is yet night, and giveth meat to her household, and a portion to her maidens. She considereth a field, and buyeth it: with the fruit of her hands she planteth a vineyard. She girdeth her loins with strength, and strengtheneth her arms. She perceiveth that her merchandise is good: her candle goeth not out by night. She layeth her hands to the spindle, and her hands hold the distaff. She stretcheth out her hand to the poor; yea, she reacheth forth her hands to the needy. She is not afraid of the snow for her household: for all her household are clothed with scarlet. She maketh herself coverings of tapestry; her clothing is silk and purple. Her husband is known in the gates, when he sitteth among the elders of the land. She maketh fine linen, and selleth it; and delivereth girdles unto the merchant. Strength and honour are her clothing; and she shall rejoice in time to come. She openeth her mouth with wisdom; and in her tongue is the law of kindness. She looketh well to the ways of her household, and eateth not the bread of idleness. Her children arise up, and call her blessed; her husband also, and he praiseth her. Many daughters have done virtuously, but thou excellest them all. Favour is deceitful, and beauty is vain: but a woman that feareth the Lord, she shall be praised.

Proverbs 31:10-30

Someone once said, "Beauty is only skin deep, but ugly goes all the way to the bone." If that's true, then virtue goes all the way to the heart.

In this last chapter of Proverbs, David and Bathsheba are writing to their son Solomon about the truth of real beauty. They're describing to him the qualities he should look for in a virtuous woman. History proves that Solomon didn't heed their advice. In fact, he had a harem of a thousand women who didn't love God. So, obviously, he had a lot of trouble on his hands. I have four females in my household, and I can't imagine having one thousand!

The Bible says one of the greatest strengths of character a wife can have is for her husband's heart to have confidence in her. And the word *virtuous* means "strong in godly character."[1] When women serve and trust God, walking in virtue and strength of character, their husbands will trust them even when they're not around.

I've talked to many couples over the years who didn't trust one another when they were apart. The first thing I ask them is "Why don't you trust your partner?" And when they answer, they recount the circumstances that resulted in betrayal and mistrust of one another. Fidelity is a trait of strength of character, or virtue. So a man or woman of virtue can be trusted.

The Bible says in 1 Peter 3:3-4 that a godly wife's adornments are not on the outside, but in the heart. The Proverbs 31 woman is a woman of great confidence, and her strength doesn't come from the spoil in her household, but from her godly character.

Have you ever known women who were really spoiled? You know the kind: If their husbands don't buy them something every week, they become angry. Then they try to manipulate him by saying, "You don't love me, because you didn't buy me this or that."

Strength of character isn't dependent upon whether or not your husband makes a lot of money. If a godly nature dwells within you, your husband will have confidence, knowing that even if he lost his job, you wouldn't self-destruct and that you would still love him. He trusts in you, knowing that no one else could walk into your life with a diamond or a ruby in his hand and sweep you off your feet.

Another characteristic of a virtuous woman is that she's never lazy or slothful. (See verse 13.) There's a desire and a drive inside her to accomplish what needs to be done for her family.

The character of a virtuous woman will drive her to do the very best she can every time she has the opportunity. Like a merchant ship, she will go out of her way to get the very best for her house. She will always do the very best she can do for her home.

Verse 15 says, **She riseth also while it is yet night, and giveth meat to her household, and a portion to her maidens.** The Spirit of God began to talk to me as I studied this verse and said, "She submits to her duty in the home. If it takes getting up early, then she gets up early. Whatever needs to get done, she's willing to do that because she's a woman of organization."

God doesn't want your life to look like your hair when you wake up in the morning. The industrious woman doesn't say, "I'm not about to get out of this bed! So what if we don't make it to church on time. Pastor doesn't start preaching until 11:30 anyway." Instead, she says, "I've got to get up early to get our children ready. I know I have things to do, and it's not easy, but I'm going to rejoice in it." Whatever needs to be done, she does it with a good attitude.

Many of us had a mother or grandmother who was up at the crack of dawn preparing breakfast for us. Do you remember that? You felt admiration for that mother or grandmother.

Now, I'm not saying you need to get up at 4:30 in the morning and start cooking to be a virtuous woman. Just do what's necessary in *your* home.

The Bible says, **She giveth meat to her household, and a portion to her maidens.** The word *portion* means she distributes, or delegates, the work.[2] During King David's time, it wasn't uncommon for people to have servants who lived with them at home. So the wife would get up, prepare the food, then go to her maidens and give them the daily "to-do" list. The quality of virtue is also blessed with abilities of organization that include a willingness to submit to personal duty and to lead when it's time to lead.

Mercy and kindness are also characteristics of virtue. (See verse 20.) Virtue doesn't produce jealousy or greediness; mercy and kindness are its traits. A woman of virtue stretches out her hand, extending mercy and kindness to everyone she meets.

As I stated earlier, women like security in the home, and they also like stability. They don't want anyone rocking the boat. When anyone or anything threatens their homes or their loved ones, they will do everything within their power to protect them. But if they live in fear, their husbands can detect it and so can their children. Women, you can't be saying, "I'm just so afraid something's going to happen." Or, "If those kids go out there and ride their bikes, they're going to fall over," because before long, your kids will be saying, "Mom, what's behind the door? I was trying to go to sleep, but I think there's a monster back there. I'm scared. Can I sleep with you?" So a virtuous woman instills faith instead of fear. Every time one of our little girls falls and scrapes her knee, Cindy says, "Let me pray for you; you're going to be healed in Jesus' name. Now, does that feel better?" That attitude demonstrated before your children instills faith.

A virtuous wife not only desires to take care of her home, but she also wants to take care of herself. When a wife is full of the glory of God, and she's glowing and radiating with confidence because she has done her part, people look at her and say, "That guy must be a good husband. He must be a good man. Look at his kids—they're in order. Look at his wife—see how happy she is. She always seems happy and full of peace. You never see her pulling her hair out." So how people see the wife will automatically cast a reflection on the whole house.

The virtuous woman works to achieve—not to just get by, but to do more than what has to be done. The Bible says she makes things with her hands and even has a surplus. She doesn't just get by—she wants to get ahead.

Because strength and honor are the clothing of a woman of virtue, the Bible says she will laugh at the days that are before her because she already knows she can handle them. She doesn't have to say, "I'm going to be a poor, little, worn-out widow one day. Without a man around, where will our food come from?" No, if that day ever comes, she will rise and shine.

When people open their mouths with virtue's wisdom and the law of kindness on their tongues, they're not moody. (See verse 26.) I know nature has a tendency to garble everyone's emotions occasionally. But by the Spirit of God, every born-again, Spirit-filled believer possesses the ability to rise up and say, "I will not be ruled by the imbalances of my body. My body is the temple of the Holy Ghost, and I make a decision to discipline my flesh, even when I don't feel like it. I will not walk in moodiness, and I will not distress my whole household. I will not disrupt my job because I don't feel good today." So wives, use wisdom, and discipline your emotions so that when you open your mouth, wisdom and kindness rule you.

Verse 30 says, **Favour is deceitful, and beauty is vain** [or passing]: **but a woman that feareth the Lord, she shall be praised.** Everything you do in word or deed, virtuous woman, you can do in the name of the Lord Jesus. You can be a virtuous wife, in the name of Jesus. You don't have to be a wife according to this world's standard. There's no reason for you to go out and struggle for honor and strength according to this world's system. You can be a woman of virtue according to the Word, if you feed on the Word of God and make a decision to care for what the Holy Ghost has given you. When you do that, your children and your husband will praise you. And others will see the qualities of the Holy Spirit shining through you.

There will be nothing in the world more satisfying to you as a woman than for people to say you're a virtuous, godly person, full of dignity, integrity, wisdom and strength.

to be—or not to be—submitted

Likewise, ye wives, be in subjection to your own husbands; that, if any obey not the word, they also

> may without the word be won by the conversation of the wives; While they behold your chaste conversation coupled with fear.
>
> 1 Peter 3:1,2

Now let's talk about true submission. In this passage of 1 Peter the word *conversation* in the Greek means "manner of life" and "totality of your ways."[3] This doesn't refer just to what you say—although your speech certainly reflects your manner of life—it also refers to the manner of life you live daily, virtuous wife.

As a wife you're not called to be in subjection to any other man on the face of this earth except your own husband. The word *subjection* in Peter's often-quoted submission passage means "in reverence or submission to."[4] It doesn't mean, "Obey everything I say. I'm your master and you're my slave." Nor does it mean, "You are to submit to me because I'm your husband." It does mean that the godly submission of a virtuous woman will witness to her ungodly husband.

I've said it numerous times—I don't blame women today who form feminist movements and spread all these other radical ideas. If I were a woman and treated the way some women are treated by men, I'd be against submission too because many times the way it's carried out is not in line with what God said. Some men treat women like they are dishrags.

Submission, according to the Word of God, deals with one thing—conversion. When women submit to their husbands, they are actually contributing to their husbands' conversions. It has nothing to do with obeying every order of the man, but it does have everything to do with obeying the Scriptures. Submission is not an action; it is an attitude of the heart.

The marriage relationship symbolizes the relationship between the church and the Lord Jesus Christ, so wives ought to do everything they do as unto the Lord. Godly submission doesn't require us to do things because Jesus came and said, "You do it or else." Jesus directs us to submit as witnesses for Him because our hearts have been melted by His love.

Remember, in the marriage relationship, God has an order. Husbands and wives have two different positions with two different responsibilities. I assure you that if somebody tries to cross that line, there will be contention and strife.

Now, let me also say this: Having a meek and a quiet spirit doesn't mean you have to be timid. Certain individuals are more vocal than others, and there's nothing wrong with that—you are who you are. But when it comes to your spirit—your character—you don't need to be a sniveling slave. The Word of God says you need to be meek, not weak. The meek are disciples; the weak, well, they're just weak!

About two-thirds of the marriage counseling I do occurs because people cease to put their trust in God. They decide to take matters into their own hands and not discipline their spirits. Consequently, this decision is manifested in a fight, an argument or a disruption of some kind. The common response is, "If I do that, he or she will just run all over me." So instead of trusting God with the situation, they fight back. I help them to develop a new trust in God, and part of that requires the development of a meek spirit. Sometimes the most powerful action you can take is to step back and let God move in the situation.

Now my wife Cindy has a few virtuous words for wives.

your place in the home
by cindy hallam

Congratulations, ladies! You have been awarded the highest honor—the role of a wife and mother. But it doesn't stop there. Women, like men, wear many different hats throughout their daily lives. And you will only wear each of them successfully when you know who you are in Christ.

How often have we heard the saying, "A woman's place is in the home"? As derogatory as that phrase has been made out to be, it really isn't. A woman's place in the home is a place of honor and privilege that women should enjoy, not shun. And Titus says the older women are to teach the younger women as models of virtuous success.

> The aged women likewise, that they be in behavior as becometh holiness, not false accusers, not given to much wine, teachers of good things; That they may teach the young women to be sober, to love their husbands, to love their children, To be discreet, chaste, keepers at home, good, obedient to their own husbands, that the word of God be not blasphemed.
>
> **Titus 2:3-5**

This passage talks about what women are to do concerning younger women and children. They are to be teachers of good things, instructing the young women to be sober and wise, to love their husbands and children, to be discreet, chaste, keepers at home and to be obedient, reverent wives.

We are called "mothers" and "women of God" for a reason. There is responsibility that goes along with those roles. We are called to teach those who are younger than us. This can include both our own natural children and spiritual children God may bring into our lives. Virtuous women, God will open doors for you to instruct others and to model the example of godliness in front of those who are younger.

As parents we can't give our children something that we don't have ourselves. If we aren't disciplined in the Word of God and are not submitted in love to one another, showing tenderness and kindness, then we can't pass on those qualities to our children.

So women, we must develop ourselves in God first. Unless we do that, we are not going to be what God has called us to be as wives or mothers. We can't expect to instill the principles of God's Word in our children if those principles haven't first been instilled in our own lives. We have to daily "practice what we teach."

When we understand that our relationships with God come first, we will be able to pass that on to our children. This is a great responsibility upon which God places great honor, and it's a pleasure and a joy to fulfill our responsibility.

If it can be avoided, don't leave your children for someone else to raise. I know that in this day and age, this isn't always feasible. In many homes, both parents must work to make ends meet, or there may be only one parent in the home. If this is your situation, please don't feel guilty. I'm speaking of those homes where the wife's salary is used for luxuries like exotic vacations, name-brand clothing, expensive cars, upper-class private lessons and so on. These are things we can do without, especially when they interfere with the raising of our children.

So when raising children, keep this thought in mind: Children are a gift from God, but ultimately they belong to Him. That makes us stewards of their lives while they live under our roofs, and we are accountable for molding, shaping and guiding them.

So do all you can do to ensure that when they're finally out of your care, they're still in God's care. Teach them the Word of God and His ways of righteousness, so that long after you're gone, they will carry out the same responsibilities with their children.

Some parents have neglected their responsibilities under the guise of freedom of choice. The excuse is, "Well, we don't want to push our religious beliefs on our children—we want to give them the opportunity to choose for themselves. When they get old enough, they'll make a quality decision to serve God in whatever church they decide is best for them." Satan is deceiving any parent who buys into this, because there is no way children are going to grow up knowing the difference between right and wrong unless somebody teaches them.

Children are learning every day of their lives, and there is no one better to teach them than a godly parent. Remember, if you're not teaching them, someone else will. The minute they walk out the front door in the morning, their friends are going to teach them all kinds of things. So will their school teachers, bus drivers and everyone with whom they come into contact.

So use your God-given authority in your children's lives every day to be their teacher and trainer. Like Hannah with Samuel, take your child to the house of God and commit him to the Lord. And show and tell him daily of God's loving reality.

Proverbs 22:6 tells us to **train up a child in the way he should go: and when he is old, he will not depart from it.** Training is showing the child what to do by demonstration; teaching is verbal instruction. So lead by example—don't just speak it, but live it too.

Virtuous woman, you have authority and control as a wife and mother, in the Spirit as well as in the natural. So do what is necessary to take your position of leadership in the home. When you do, your husband will be supported to fulfill his leadership role and your children will grow up strong in the admonition of the Lord.

foundations for a godly home

God has a way of putting a house together so the winds of this life can't blow it apart. But there are two ways you can choose to live. Whether you are currently raising your family or your family is already raised doesn't matter. You can choose to do it the world's way, or you can choose to do it God's way. The world's way is a hit-and-miss proposition, but God's ways are never wrong.

Cindy and I are on a crusade for the family because the Word of God speaks a great deal about the Christian family and the covenant that God has with us. Jesus made a covenant that has been sealed with His blood. It's a covenant with you, your family and your household.

Families are being destroyed because they lack a covenant with God. It's not that God Himself is lacking in any way, but His covenant is lacking in many homes that He greatly desires to bless.

Love will come supernaturally to a family when they recognize that God is the One who made the covenant. When you make a decision to not walk in the counsel of the ungodly and to hear what God has to say about marriage and family, His love will be expressed in your actions and attitudes.

give me the truth!

Many times people put too much stock in the emotional side of love because that's all the world has to offer. But no one can stay emotionally high on anything indefinitely. That's wonderful when you're dating; your feet haven't touched the ground yet—you don't even need to eat! But as soon as you get married, your appetite cuts loose, and you start eating everything in the house!

Joshua 24:14 says, **Now therefore fear the Lord, and serve him in sincerity and in truth....** This verse reveals two important qualities that are extremely necessary in a godly home—sincerity and truth.

I like Joshua because he talks like a man of God. He had his house so in order that he could speak for his household when he said, "You can serve whomever you want, but choose this day whom you will serve (at least make a declaration of something). But as for me and my house, we're going to serve God." (See Joshua 24:14.) He was truly a godly husband and father who did what was necessary to say, "I and my house love God, and we will always serve Him."

Thank God for men and women who say, "We're not just going part of the way with the covenant. We're not just going to serve God occasionally. We will continually serve the Lord, and we will declare it. We will serve Him with sincerity, and we will serve Him with truth."

grafted into the family vine

How deep do your family roots go? Can you trace them? If you can, did your family leave you an inheritance—not just a financial inheritance, but a spiritual one as well, with basic moral values?

There are four areas in the following passage regarding a covenant family: financial blessing, happiness, a blessed spouse and blessed children.

> **Blessed is every one that feareth the Lord; that walketh in his ways. For thou shalt eat the labour of thine hands: happy shalt thou be, and it shall be well with thee. Thy wife shall be as a fruitful vine by the sides of thine house: thy children like olive plants round about thy table. Behold, that thus shall the man be blessed that feareth the Lord. The Lord shall bless thee out of Zion: and thou shalt see the good of Jerusalem all the days of thy life. Yea, thou shalt see thy children's children, and peace upon Israel.**
>
> **Psalm 128**

financial blessings

This psalm says the blessed man and woman who walk in covenant relationship have said yes to serving Jesus together. "Yes, we're going to walk uprightly." And verse 2 says they are going to eat the labor of their hands. In other words, they will be successful financially. Don't say, "I have a million dollars, and that means God made me rich." That's not necessarily the case, because God doesn't always promise that we will become multimillionaires; that is not even how God judges success. He has streets of gold and huge pearly gates, so a million dollars to God is like chicken feed.

Many times God does give a million dollars to people because He wants to use it to accomplish godly purposes in their lives. But a million dollars is not the end result of what God wants to give. This is why often when people become blessed with a little money, they start hoarding it, not realizing that God desires to bless them even more.

The Word of God is His manual for using money. Every believer should tithe to promote God's work. And everyone should save money, even if it's a little at a time. You say, "Why should we save money? Don't you believe that Jesus is coming back?" Absolutely, I believe Jesus is coming back. But we also need to plan for emergency situations by putting money away in savings accounts or in retirement funds.

Saving is not a matter of how much you contribute; it's a lifestyle. Once you begin to save a little money, you will find yourself feeding that habit. Start with a quarter or fifty cents if you have to, but do it regularly.

happiness

Verse 2 of this psalm talks about happiness. But you can't buy happiness with money. Happiness comes when you have maintained the terms of the covenant. God says, **Happy shalt thou be, and it shall be well with thee.** Happiness is a beautiful quality that God gives you. It comes because circumstances and conditions are right, but it is not to be confused with joy, a fruit of the Spirit. Joy comes because the Spirit of God gives it to you. You can have joy in the middle of a storm, like Paul and Silas, who had joy even when they had been beaten and locked up in prison.

You too can laugh and sing joyfully in the face of adversity or difficult circumstances. *Happiness* is conditional based upon the circumstances, whereas *joy* is conditional only based upon the attitude of the heart. And God will make you happy! But along with God's happiness there are some conditions and circumstances that must line up with His plan.

God doesn't want you to fake happiness—He wants you to actually experience happiness. He wants circumstances and conditions to be right so the attitude of your mind is the same as the attitude of your heart.

Second Kings 4 tells about a Shunammite woman who believed God for a son. And God answered her prayers. But one day the son went out to work in the field with his daddy, and he became ill. The father didn't have any faith; it was the mom who was the believer. The father came back and brought the boy home to his mother, and the boy died in her lap.

So she said, "Saddle up one of the donkeys; I'm going to see the man of God."

When she found Elisha's servant, he said, "How is everything? How is it with your son? How is it with your husband? How is it with your home?"

And she said, "All is well."

Now, you know that she had a dead boy lying in her house, but here's a woman who had a covenant, and she believed her son had come from God. She had already made a decision and said, "I don't care what comes, I want the plan of God. My household will be happy, and everything is going to be well no matter how many attacks the devil tries to put on us. I will *not* change my confession. If the covenant doesn't change, I'm not going to change." So she confessed with her mouth and believed in her heart that all was well. And as you continue reading her story you'll see that Elisha learned what had happened and raised her boy from the dead. (See 2 Kings 4:27-37.)

I'd like to tell you, the covenant will not change in a family if you will walk in the covenant of the Lord Jesus. Even in the face of insurmountable odds, speak the plan of God into action in your family. Teach your children, also, to confess God's promises.

blessed spouse

Psalm 128:3 says, **Thy wife shall be as a fruitful vine by the sides of thine house.** That's a tremendous statement. God says He will bless your marriage relationship, and your wife will be like a fruitful vine by the sides of your house. The NIV says, **Your wife will be like a fruitful vine within your house.**

As Cindy described so well in the last chapter, the wife and mother has a tremendous place of respect, endearment and honor in a covenant family home. In today's society, if a woman is a housewife, some people tend to think something is wrong with her. If she's not pressing every way she can to climb the corporate ladder or have an illustrious career, she's often looked down upon for being *just* a wife.

A "fruitful vine" is a productive vine, so the psalmist could be talking about having children in this verse. If you want to have children and you're having problems conceiving, Jesus can heal you and give you your heart's desire. But being fruitful also means you'll prosper in the home. When you are fruitful you will be the best wife, the best employee, the best mother or the best minister of the gospel inside and outside of the home.

blessed children

...thy children like olive plants round about thy table (v. 3).

Olives are very unique, and they come from some of the longest living trees. The oldest tree in Israel is over two thousand years old. They say that particular tree was there when Jesus walked on the face of the earth. Possibly He sat under that tree, and it's still alive—that's phenomenal.

The Bible says your children will be like olive plants around your table. God wants your children to live to a "ripe, old age." Begin to pray what God says about your children. I confess over my children and pray that all of my children will outlive me if the Rapture doesn't happen first. Thank God that He will satisfy them with long life and show them His salvation.

The second truth about an olive tree is that it is extremely fruitful and bears fruit for a long, long time. Likewise, not only are our children going to live a long time, but they will bear fruit and be witnesses—even in their old age.

Thirdly, Jesus personally used olive trees while He was on the earth. He used them for shade and for illustration in His parables. And when Jesus went away to escape the crowds, He went to the Mount of Olives. So Jesus will also use your children. There's no greater security in life than knowing that your children love God and are being used of God. The Bible says He guides the steps of our righteous young ones into joy and lights their paths in front of them.

The fact that Psalm 128 also talks about being around the table indicates unity. One of the most precious times in our home is when we sit down at the table together. We lead an active lifestyle, and I'm sure you do too. We're always on the go, and many times we have to eat out. But we've curtailed eating out in order to have more time around our table as a family.

When your children sit down with you somewhere, however, they should be a blessing to you and not a curse. Family time shouldn't be "wrestle mania" night. There should be godly conversation, joy and happiness when you sit down together at the table. Instead of fighting over the last biscuit, children in a godly home should be thanking God that they have plenty to eat. We take turns saying the blessing, and I often have to be careful which one I call on—depending upon how hungry I am—because my children love to thank God for the blessings He has given us!

You may want your child to grow up to be a doctor, a lawyer, an astronaut or a professional athlete, but there's something wonderful about allowing God to use your children in whatever way He chooses. Turn them over to Jesus and confess in His name that they can only be what God has destined for them to become.

Part III

Three Lifelines
in Marriage

lifeline #1: communication

In the next three chapters I want to talk about what I call covenant marriage lifelines that help connect the tupperware-china gap. The first one I want to mention is communication—the very lifeline of a relationship. Just as hardening of the arteries prevents the flow of blood in your body, so a lack of communication will lead to the death of your marriage and family relationships. So, there are communication skills that will make you a success in a marriage, at a job or anywhere else in life. And for the most part, they can all be summed up in one sentence in the book of James.

> **Wherefore, my beloved brethren, let every man be swift to hear, slow to speak, slow to wrath.**
>
> **James 1:19**

The book of James has much to say about the tongue, the most vital tool of human communication. In the third chapter, James says if you can control your tongue, you can control your entire environment—body, soul and spirit. Some people have what I call "hoof-in-mouth" disease, which means they speak twice as much as they listen.

So, the first area of communication we need to practice is learning to be swift to hear, according to James 1. *Swift to hear* means that you're "always listening." In a family relationship, what you have to say is not nearly as important as your willingness to listen. James says, "Be swift to hear and slow to speak." The emphasis is on *swift* and *slow.*

Communication comes in two different ways: verbal and nonverbal. Verbal communication is important; it's the most obvious form of communication. Men and women need to learn not to take one another for granted, but to be willing to give the other person all the respect they would want to receive themselves. Listening builds self-esteem, but shutting people out humiliates them. When you are swift to hear, you learn how to listen. And learning how to listen is as important as learning how to talk. There are many ways to listen without using your ears. You listen with your entire attitude, including your body language. The way you sit, stand, walk and talk are all nonverbal signals to other people of how attentive you are to what they are saying.

Listening was one of the first things you learned when you became a Christian. You heard God's voice calling you to repentance, and when you came into the kingdom of God, He immediately started fine tuning your ear to hear the voice of the Spirit. He began fine-tuning your mind to receive the Word of God so faith could dwell in your heart.

I heard what you did not say

So often, Christians try to exercise control over one another by not paying attention or listening attentively to what the other person is saying. Their nonverbal communication, or body language, sometimes speaks louder than their words.

Your eyes are communicators. You can look at somebody squarely in the eye and know if he or she is truly listening to you. Someone once said that the eyes are the windows to the soul—and that's so true. You can look in people's eyes and almost tell what they are thinking.

Your hands and arms also speak volumes when you're communicating. One of the most important interviewing tips ever given is to make direct eye contact and give a firm handshake before and after the interview. This is important because first impressions are lasting ones. The same advice can be applied to any situation.

Usually when people sit in front of you with their arms crossed, it means they aren't really interested in what you have to say. How often have you begun a conversation that escalates into a heated debate, and suddenly you (or the other person) begin waving your arms around like a madman? What you're saying to the other person is "I'm not sure I want to listen to this anymore...get out of my face or else!" Or maybe you're talking and before long, you start clenching your fists. Some people clench their fists when they get frustrated and angry.

Husbands and wives, you need to make a decision right now to *not* shut one another out. When was the last time you asked your mate to sit down with you for a talk, for no reason other than just to share with each other? Make a decision to listen to each other. Listening builds tremendous self-image in a family, and it gives tremendous credibility to your position in the home as a wife or a husband.

Do you remember when you were dating, before you were married, how you listened to everything that was good, and you couldn't see or hear anything bad about that person? Ladies, remember when you were dating your husband, and all he talked about was golf? You couldn't have cared less about golf, but you said, "That's really interesting. So you nail birdies? That's wonderful. The only place you get to shoot eagles is on the golf course? That's amazing! Don't you need a license to shoot eagles and birdies?"

The same is true for men. Remember, it made no difference what she talked about—she could talk about cooking a roast, and we men would say, "That's amazing! I never saw a roast look so good in my life." Then you got married—and your ears fell off. Now, that's amazing! But, the Bible says you must be swift to listen.

Attitudes also speak louder than words. Somebody once said, "I heard what you did not say." Many times, unspoken attitudes will say more than words ever could. When you're swift to listen, not only will you detect attitudes that you may not otherwise see, but you'll also be curious about why that person is reacting that way. You may say, "Well, he's just in one of those moods again." Or, "I don't know what's the matter with her. She just gets that way every now and then." Neither one of these attitudes is a legitimate reason to overlook how you are treating your mate.

If you have a desire to love your spouse as Christ loved the church, you'll find out why he or she reacts in those ways.

You will begin to minister to your spouse in the area where he or she is hurting, and you will help turn him or her around.

So be attentive. One of the greatest things you can do when you are having a conversation with your spouse is to look him or her in the eye. When you make eye contact with your mate, you demonstrate to him or her that what is being said is important, that your mate is valuable to you and that you respect him or her.

if the turkey leg fits, leave it on

Christian men, you can choose to be free of the limitations placed on you from the time you were born. And this is good because people often need to break free of old habits in their family relationships. Some men treat their wives the same way their fathers treated their mothers, which was the way Grandpa treated Grandma and Great-Grandpa treated Great-Grandma. The cycle was repeated generation after generation. Those traits have been in the family for as long as they can remember—but both men and women can change.

I once heard a story about a lady who, before cooking a big, juicy turkey, would cut off one of the legs and cook it separately. One day she had friends over for supper, and as she was preparing to cook the turkey, she cut the leg off one side before she put it in the oven. Curiosity was nearly killing an onlooking guest, until finally the friend said, "I want to ask you a question. Why did you cut off one of the drumsticks before putting the bird in the oven?"

"Well, I don't know. That's just the way my mother used to do it," the lady answered hesitantly.

The curiosity bug bit the hostess, too. So the next day she asked her mother, "Mother, why do you cut the leg off the turkey before you cook it?"

The mother thought about it for a while and answered, "Well, I don't know. That's the way my grandma did it."

So they asked the grandmother. "Grandma, why did you cut the leg off of the turkey before cooking it?"

"Well, our stove was so small when we were growing up that the turkey wouldn't fit in there," grandma casually replied. "So we cut off one of the legs so it would fit."

Many people are like the gracious hostess and her mother in many areas of their lives—blindly doing things a particular way simply because "that's the way it's always been done." They've learned poor character and relationship skills that have been passed down for generations. Maybe at one time there was some merit to following those particular habits, but often there is no logical reason to continue the pattern.

I've heard many people say, "I've got a quick temper—but five minutes later, I'm not angry anymore. I'm not even worried about it. I vent my frustrations and then—poof— they're gone." But, if this is you, after the dust settles, you've left wounded people behind you. Why should you worry about it? Because you've done serious damage to your husband or wife and your children. You've slaughtered their self-esteem and self-worth with the flick of your tongue.

Defensiveness is a learned attitude—a terrible trait that is a result of pride. One way to break defensiveness is to be willing to accept godly, constructive criticism. But some people are so full of false pride that if their spouses try to help them see the truth, they refuse to believe it. So always be willing to practice James' teaching of being slow to anger, and the love of God will take over your life.

two words to avoid

I mentioned this lifeline principle just a little earlier, but let's focus on it now. Remember the two words you should not use in your marriage or your home: *always* and *never.* Have you ever caught yourself saying, "You *always* do that, and every time I turn around, you're *always* doing the same thing"? Or, "You *never* do what I ask you to do. You're *never* going to amount to anything—you're *always* going to be a loser"? When you lash out with harsh words in a fit of anger or frustration, you can't take them back. They create images that will remain in the listener's memory bank for years to come, especially if hurled at a child. Children are known for their resilience and ability to forgive quickly. But even so, you impact their self-image by what comes out of your mouth.

Whatever you speak to your children, they are guaranteed to fulfill in their lives. "You're always in trouble." That's exactly right, and they're going to stay in trouble because they were taught to believe that lie. I'm not saying that children can't overcome those negative thoughts. But chances become greater that they won't, because the most important people in their lives—their parents—have imbedded into their psyche the idea that they can't do anything right, and they grow up believing they can't. So *always* and *never* can be damaging words, particularly when they're "dumped."

no dumping allowed

Have you ever seen signs that say "No Dumping Allowed"? A dump is full of garbage and unusable things that have been thrown together—orange peels, banana peels, empty cans, milk cartons, newspapers and all kinds of junk. In personal relationships there is emotional garbage, and the same rule applies: "No Dumping Allowed!" For example, you might be discussing a particular thing with your mate, and, during the course of the conversation, you bring up something from the past that is totally irrelevant to the subject at hand.

Introducing such a point is often done to strengthen or emphasize an opposing position—but it's not fair to dig up old garbage! If you're going to be slow to anger in your relationships, make a decision not to "dump" on other people, especially your family members. Decide to link your thoughts together so that your two-way communication is more effective. Stay in the now. Keep the garbage in the past.

what's the real problem?

Another breakdown in communication occurs when people associate a small dislike with a major rip in a relationship, particularly in the marriage relationship. Too many husbands and wives major on minors by turning small, insignificant things into big problems. "I don't like the way you cooked that cornbread. That's the problem—it's the cornbread. I've told you I don't like that much salt in it, and you put too much salt in it all the time. That's the problem with our marriage."

Take a step back and look at this logically. This guy just associated too much salt in the cornbread with the reason his marriage wasn't working. Wrong! Instead of making a mountain out of insignificant incidents, he should have found out the real reason his marriage wasn't working. A good place to start would be to look inside himself.

Like David, we should all ask for the Lord's help:

> **Search me, O God, and know my heart.... See if there is any offensive way in me.**
>
> **Psalm 139:23,24 NIV**

A good place to begin is by examining your own life to see if you said or did anything to provoke a negative reaction in your mate. As the saying goes, "It takes two to tango," and arguments and problems are rarely ever just one person's fault.

don't bring witchcraft into the home

Manipulation is a negative technique that is sometimes used in communication. Manipulation is a spirit of control—a "Jezebel spirit"—and is considered witchcraft. That's why manipulation is so distasteful—because it's associated with witchcraft. It involves a variety of facets—including both verbal and nonverbal communication.

Many people try to manipulate others nonverbally. For instance, they may turn and walk out in the middle of a conversation. Following after them, the other person may say, "Don't walk away from me. Why are you leaving? I don't understand why you're leaving." The manipulative person doesn't really want to leave the other person; he or she is simply trying to get his or her own way by walking out.

Here's a classic case of manipulation: You're talking to somebody, and when the conversation gets out of hand, this person heaves a long, drawn-out sigh. It nearly crushes you, doesn't it? Or how about frowning? In order to let the other person know where you're coming from, you give them *the look*. These forms of manipulation are used to try to gain control of another person without giving him or her the dignity of communicating verbally—and they always produce anger.

silence is not always golden

Then there's the silent treatment. There are times when silence is not golden, and conflict management is one of those times. It's one thing to remain silent because you fear the repercussions your words will have before you've thought them through. But it's quite another to use silence as a form of manipulation to gain control of another person. Ultimately, this type of manipulation drives a wedge between husbands and wives instead of drawing them closer together. For example, if a wife uses the silent treatment on her husband, he gets the impression that she is not interested in him, so he thinks, *Why should I bother to ask what's wrong? It doesn't matter what I say; she's still going to ignore me.*

Communication in any relationship is a vital lifeline—a main artery—to the life of that relationship. So avoid all the mentioned communication pitfalls in this chapter. And remember, the success of your marriage and home depend on God and godly communication. Without establishing good communication in your marriage, all other aspects, including intimacy, financial success and godly parenting of your children, will collapse. But when communication is flowing between you, life will also flow and the blessings of God will overtake your family.

lifeline #2: sex and intimacy

In this chapter I want to look at our second marital lifeline, sex. You know as well as I do that the mentality of society today is "If it feels good, do it." So a basic question that is commonly asked by potential marriage partners is "How can I know if we're sexually compatible if we don't live together first?" Unfortunately, this kind of self-serving philosophy ultimately causes the breakdown of marriages, leaving children as the victims.

Before entering into a sexual relationship, which God created for the confines of marriage, a couple should spend adequate time in developing intimacy and good communication skills. We've already established that communication is as vital to a successful marriage as blood is to life. Without communication, you don't even have a relationship; and without the intimacy of a sacred marriage relationship, you just coexist, which is what "shacking up," or living together, is.

Intimacy, on the other hand, can be a shared premarital experience without the act of sex. Intimacy is not the perverted concept that is prevalent in today's society. True intimacy is a deep level of communication, and you must have it to have a great sex life. Marriage is a school of character that trains us how to get along together—preferably, Jesus' way. The devil will do everything in his power to undermine and destroy godly marriages. He tempts one or both of the marriage partners to become involved in adultery, pornography, lust and all manner of promiscuous sin. And if he can get them to sin, he separates people from the will of God.

So, when it comes to your marriage, take the utmost care to control your thoughts. Learn to listen to your spirit and become an expert in God's Word. Don't let your mind or your emotions control you. Don't let others on the job tell you how to conduct your marriage relationship. If their ideas were so great, things would be working better in their own marriages.

You can't help it when thoughts pop into your head, but you can control whether or not those thoughts become actions. You can take dominion over your thought life through the power of God. AMEN !

a three-legged race

> **Two are better than one; because they have a good reward for their labour.**
>
> **Ecclesiastes 4:9**

I believe Solomon was speaking about spiritual labor in this verse. The first way to develop intimacy is to have a spiritual union. Husbands and wives are called together to work for the Lord. God's calling on your life as an individual will not, and should not, separate you from your mate. Do something together in Jesus' name. Whether it's passing out tracts or visiting the sick in the hospital—do it together. There's a tremendous strength in couples who work together for God.

A strong bridge is built in a couple's relationship when they are not embarrassed or ashamed to work together and speak the name of Jesus openly to one another.

I've had ladies tell me, "God told me to marry this man. I know God sent him into my life." My first thought when I hear this is usually *They should know better because they claim to have been Spirit-filled for longer than I've been around.* Then I ask, "Does this man go to church?"

"Well, no, but he's a Christian," they reply.

Strike one!

"Has this man ever been filled with the Holy Ghost?" I ask next.

"Well, no," they answer. "But, he's not against it, and I have told him that I am Spirit-filled and speak in tongues, and he thinks that's okay."

Strike two! (At this stage, they're batting zero.)

I figure if their man has at least been to church, then there may be some hope for the relationship. So, the next question I've asked is "Has this man ever been to church with you before?"

"Well, not really," they say. "I met him in a bowling league, but he doesn't forbid me to come to church."

Strike three!

Before long, they say, "We're getting married, Pastor. I don't care what you say."

I reply, "Okay. That's between you and God."

You're out! These women are out of their minds for pursuing marriage with this kind of men. And before you know it, they're out of the church too, because, let's face it, they will eventually stop coming if their husbands don't attend. It's unlikely that I see them in church twice a year after they tie the knot. Sad, but true.

Don't settle for less than God's best. Listen, if you're dating someone who isn't converted before marriage, what makes you think you can convert him or her afterwards? There is no such thing as "missionary dating." It doesn't work, because it's not biblical. It's not God's way.

Perhaps you became a Christian after you married, and because of it, your unbelieving mate left. In time, one of two things may happen: Your mate may decide he or she wants to come back—at which time you will have to prayerfully decide whether to receive him or her back. Or, God may send someone else into your life, so the choice is always yours.

Somebody once compared marriage to a three-legged race. You have two people—each one bound to the other by one leg—trying to work together toward a common goal using their unbound legs. They run—stumbling, fumbling and falling down along the way—but they keep getting up and going on.

In *Making Your Husband Feel Loved,* Betty Malz shared a story told by Evelyn Roberts, about how she and her husband, Oral Roberts, developed intimacy through the years.

> Our marriage has been special because both of us have worked at it. But at least one time I didn't work hard enough to see his [Oral's] real needs.

In the early days of our crusades, I couldn't always go with him because of the children. So just before Oral came home, Rebecca, our oldest daughter, and I would sit down and plan the meals we would have when her dad came home.... A few evenings after his homecoming from one of these trips, Oral said to me, "Evelyn, put the children to bed. I want to talk to you." When the children were tucked in bed, I joined him in the den and closed the door.

He said, "Evelyn, there's something wrong with our marriage."

My eyebrows flew up. "There is?"

"Yes," he said. "You haven't paid any attention to me since I've been home. It's like I don't exist. You spend time with the children, but none with me."

"Oral," I replied, not at all calmly, "I have spent hours fixing your favorite foods. I have asked the children to be on their best behavior and let you rest. I've tried so hard to please you. Honey, you are gone so much you don't know what a normal marriage is like."

He said, "I don't want a normal marriage. I want an above normal marriage—the best anyone has ever had!"

Well, as you can imagine, there was a lot of apologizing, kissing, hugging and lovemaking that night, for I realized that, even though I hadn't know[n] it before, he felt I was ignoring him.

Since then I have learned that no matter what I feel in my heart for my husband, unless I tell him and show him in ways he can understand, he really doesn't know I love him.[1] *Interesting*

Evelyn Roberts knows the secret to intimacy: showing her husband, Oral, how much she loves him in ways he can understand. She communicates her love for him by doing and saying those things that mean the most to *him*. Through open communication, Evelyn and her husband meet each other's needs and develop an intimate relationship. Oral and Evelyn Roberts know what it means to run a "three-legged race."

The marriage relationship is an eternal relationship made up of two imperfect people who have to learn how to work together. Spiritually, a bond is formed between the two that can't be broken. If that tie is strong, the devil can't break through it, no matter how hard he tries.

First, develop a spiritual relationship; and a soulish, or emotional, relationship will follow in its rightful place.

> **For if they fall, the one will lift up his fellow: but woe to him that is alone when he falleth; for he hath not another to help him up.**
> **Ecclesiastes 4:10**

There is an emotional level that shouldn't be shared with any other than Jesus or your mate. Some men begin to share their deepest emotions with other women they know— coworkers, close friends, acquaintances, their secretaries or even waitresses at restaurants. If one of these women listens attentively and begins to "mother" the man, the two often become emotionally bonded to such a degree that the man thinks he can no longer relate to his wife.

Be a caring person, but stay within the boundaries of the Word of God. Misery has always loved company—and still does—but the only worthwhile company for misery is the Spirit and the Word. *Well, alright*

✓ If you and your mate are walking in unity and one of you falls, the other will be right there to pick the other up. But if one becomes so wrapped up with his or her own ideas and work that developing a relationship with the other is neglected, this won't be the case. Eventually, when one begins to stumble emotionally, the other won't even know he or she is hurting. *✓*

All the signs may be there—the stress, the fatigue, the loneliness—but they go unnoticed. Then one of them walks into the home one day and his or her mate is gone. "I don't know what happened," he says. "Everything was fine yesterday, but I came home today and she is gone. I don't know why."

Well, all the warning signs were there—you were just too involved in your own world to notice. Did you talk? Did you communicate? Did you learn what made him mad? Did you notice she was unhappy and try to find out why? Did you develop an intimate relationship? No, you didn't, or you would have known.

One of the keys to increasing intimacy is developing the ability to listen and disagree without interrupting. Let your mate finish his or her thought. Some husbands and wives can't say more than half a sentence at a time because the other person wants to finish it for him or her. The moment one tries to speak, the other jumps down his or her throat. This produces strife. (But listening and not cutting off the other person in midstream is a form of respect.)

Another way you listen is with your body language. Ladies, men often have trouble expressing exactly how they feel, but you can often figure it out by the way they hold themselves. Watch and observe him—how he walks, sits and conducts himself. If he is discouraged or upset, your attentive eyes and ears can be a great booster to his ego. Let him know you care by your look and your actions. Little things mean a lot, so write him a love note and place it where he will find it. Take him a cool beverage if he's working in the yard or the garage. Prepare his favorite snack and sit down to share it with him while he watches television.

And men, flowers aren't just for funerals, anniversaries and Valentine's Day. Bring your wife's favorite flower home, and watch her whole face light up. If she's had a long day at work, offer to take her out to dinner and a movie. If the kids are driving her nuts, get a baby-sitter for the weekend and whisk her away to some unknown destination. It doesn't have to be extravagant—a simple one-day excursion will do. Anything to get her out of the house!

Intimacy is also learning to enjoy each other's company and laughing together. I'm always cutting up with Cindy, and she's always cutting up with me—it's great! Live joyfully! Make a decision to smile at your spouse at least once a day, whether he or she seems to need it or not. Don't you remember how happy you were when you were dating? Well, you're still the same person. You may have changed some, but you're basically the same person, and so is your spouse. So keep joy in your relationship—and don't take yourselves so seriously!

Intimacy takes discipline, and you don't instantaneously become intimate just because you're married. God wants you to experience intimacy and learn how to communicate with one another. So sit down together to talk and listen. Discuss things. Talk with your eyes. Talk with your hands. Talk with your time. Develop hobbies and fun activities to do together, because finding things to do and enjoy with one another will increase intimacy.

one + one = one

After developing the spiritual and emotional aspects of your relationship, you will have less trouble developing the physical aspect. But it won't happen overnight simply because you are husband and wife.

> **Also, if two lie down together, they will keep warm. But how can one keep warm alone?**
> **Ecclesiastes 4:11** NIV

A lot of people struggle in marriage with their physical, sexual relationship, but that's not the plan of God. He doesn't want a husband and wife to struggle with sex in their covenant marriage relationship. God wants you to have a healthy, godly, sexual relationship. The longer you stay married, the more enjoyable the physical part of your lives should become. The physical aspect of the relationship should be a natural by-product of your love for one another that has been developed spiritually and emotionally. ✓

> **Marriage is honorable in all, and the bed undefiled: but whoremongers and adulterers God will judge.**
> **Hebrews 13:4**

We see clearly in the Bible that the sexual relationship in marriage is something extremely honorable and precious in the sight of God. Sex was given by God for two reasons. First, it was given to procreate, or to continue the family of God. Secondly, it was given for affection, love and enjoyment between a husband and wife. Sex is for marriage only. God calls any sexual activity outside of marriage lasciviousness, harlotry, adultery and fornication—and He says those who commit these sins will not enter into the kingdom of heaven. (See 1 Corinthians 6:9.) So, if you think God doesn't demand purity, holiness, righteousness and sanctification in your marriage, you are greatly deceived.

Our text in Hebrews says marriage is honorable. The word *honorable* in the Greek means "valuable, extremely costly or highly esteemed."[2] So, God says marriage is valuable, extremely costly and highly esteemed. And He says the marriage bed must be undefiled. The word *undefiled* means "pure or unsoiled."[3] There are some people who, when they first get saved, think they can't have sexual relationships with their spouses because it's unholy. But the good news is that God says a proper sexual relationship is holy because it typifies the union of the body of Christ *with* Christ.

The Word of God deals in 1 Corinthians 7 with the marriage relationship. Paul addresses how a man is to act toward a woman, and a woman toward a man. When we fail to follow biblical instruction in this area, problems and negative responses can arise.

"Well, she's not fulfilling her duties as a wife." "He's not sensitive enough." The excuses can mount up. So, let's use the Word of God as a thermometer and see how hot or cold we are according to the Word.

The first thing you need to understand is that your body belongs to God. Before anything, or anybody else—even a wife or husband—your body belongs to God; it is the temple of the Holy Ghost.

> **What? know ye not that your body is the temple of the Holy Ghost which is in you, which ye have of God, and ye are not your own? For ye are bought with a price: therefore glorify God in your body, and in your spirit, which are God's.**
>
> 1 Corinthians 6:19,20

You aren't your own, because you have been bought with a price. So, you belong to God first, and then you are shared with a man or a woman in marriage. That's why the bed needs to be honorable and undefiled. That's why all types of perverse and outlandish sexual activity are sin and a stench in the nostrils of God. Anything that would degrade or prostitute the body in any way is a sin toward God, because your body is the temple of the Holy Ghost. You'd be surprised how many times I've counseled people, and one of the partners wanted to be involved in some strange sexual perversion. The reasoning behind it was "Well, the Bible says the bed is unde-filed, and what we do behind our doors is between us." But they're wrong, because what we do with our bodies is *first* between us and God, and *then* between our marital mates.

Paul was very clear regarding the man and woman's sexual role in marriage.

> **Let the husband render unto the wife due benevo-lence: and likewise also the wife unto the husband.**
> **1 Corinthians 7:3**

The word *render* comes from a Greek word that means "to give away."[4] So Paul tells men to love their wives and cherish them as the finest things in their households. Men, your wife isn't an object; she is a human being who is the temple of the Holy Ghost. God says she is more valuable than you are. So, as a husband, you are to freely distribute to her due benevolence. The word *benevolence* in the Greek means "good will."[5] God didn't say to hold out on, intimidate, manipulate or force yourself in any way upon your wife. He said you are to give yourself away to her as Christ freely gave His life for His bride, the church.

I'm convinced that God intends for the husband to be the leading partner in the sexual relationship of the home. Men, don't expect your wife to be "Miss Everything." God says *you* are to be the man of your house, with a heart of goodwill toward your wife. And, He says you are to love her with pure affection.

Ladies, the same goes for you:

> ...likewise also the wife [render due benevolence] unto the husband. The wife hath not power of her own body, but the husband: and likewise also the husband hath not power of his own body, but the wife.
>
> 1 Corinthians 7:3,4

The word *power* in this verse comes from the tense of the Greek word *exousia,* from which we get our English word "ability." It's a term that means "to hold power over something or to rule with power."[6] (See 1 Corinthians 6:12.) Be willing to freely give yourself to your husband in love, not in manipulation.

There's nothing as frustrating to a wife or husband as a spouse who tries to use his or her body as leverage to obtain something from his or her mate. There needs to be a willingness involved in your decision to submit yourself sexually to your mate. A heart of subjection loves and gives freely in every aspect of life.

The only time you should refrain from any sexual activity is when both partners consent to it for the purpose of prayer—and even then only for a time, not indefinitely. Paul writes: **Defraud ye not one the other, except it be with consent for a time** (1 Cor. 7:5).

To *defraud* means "to deprive or to hold back through a fraudulent or a conniving manner."[7] The word *consent* is the word *sunphonos* in the Greek, from which we get our word *symphony.* And a symphony is an orchestra in harmony.[8]

God says if you have consented to give yourself to fasting and prayer for a period of time, you should come together again so Satan can't tempt you for lack of self-restraint. (See verse 5.) Understand your limits and your motives.

Put your heart and soul into making your marriage work, and the intimacy and fulfillment of a healthy sexual relationship will follow. Without intimacy and the river of the Holy Spirit flowing in your marriage, you will never experience what it really means to be "husband and wife." What God has joined together, let no one (including *you*) put asunder.

lifeline #3: finances

The number one problem in marriages today is not actually sex or a lack of communication; it's our third marital lifeline connection—finances. No wonder God has over two thousand Scriptures in the Bible dealing on some level with His solution to our financial problems: giving.

There's no sin in having money, as long as money doesn't have you. So the first principle that can help you receive and enjoy financial prosperity in your home is that the attitude of your heart will determine the success in your life. The Bible says in Proverbs 4:23, **Keep thy heart with all diligence; for out of it are the issues of life.** In the parable of the sower found in Mark 4:19, Jesus tells us that when seed is sown, it begins to grow, but if deceitfulness grows along with the seed, it chokes out the Word.

> **And these are they which are sown among thorns; such as hear the word, And the cares of this world, and the deceitfulness of riches, and the lusts of other things entering in, choke the word, and it becometh unfruitful.**
> **Mark 4:18,19**

So as Jesus teaches, riches can be either a great deceiver or a great servant.

Another financial principle is that you must retain honesty and integrity before God with your money. Ananias and Sapphira sold a piece of land and then came before God bringing only a part of the price, when they had obviously made a covenant to bring *all* of it.

> A certain man named Ananias, with Sapphira his wife, sold a possession, and kept back part of the price, his wife also being privy to it, and brought a certain part, and laid it at the apostles' feet.
>
> Acts 5:1,2

Verses 3-11 of Acts 5 say that because Satan filled Ananias and Sapphira's hearts with the love of money, they lied to the Holy Ghost, and judgment fell on them.

I learned a long time ago to be very honest with God when it comes to my finances, because my heart, first of all, wants to be honest toward God. Our family gives at least 30 percent of our cash income into the ministry, and we have done so for several years. We started with 10 percent, moved up to 20 percent and then moved up to 30 percent. Someday we just may live on 10 percent and give the other 90 percent to God! You say, "You must be very well off to do that." Not really, but I'm rich in the Spirit.

We train our children this way because we want them to walk in prosperity. My parents taught me to be honest with God when it comes to finances. They said, "Son, if you go out and mow a yard and you make ten dollars, put back one dollar for God. If you need to, bring me that one dollar, and I'll hold it for you until you can put it in the offering."

Now we have three "Hallamite" daughters, and I tell them, "Now, if you get a dollar, you need to save ten cents for God. And if you need me to, I'll hold it for you until you can give it in the offering." But I don't have to do that very often, because they've been properly trained. They go to youth services where the teaching they receive reinforces giving and honesty before God.

The next time you start to give in an offering and the devil tries to tell you that you don't have enough money to give, just give it all. He will never again tell you that you don't have enough money to give! And God will never abandon you. Just do it in faith. If the devil knows that when he tries to push you, you're just going to push back in the Holy Ghost, he will stop and go look for someone else.

Another important point regarding honesty is that you must never cheat other people. If you make a decision never to rob God or cheat other people, your marriage will be blessed with a tremendous amount of trust. It's incredible how much trust is built when an individual says, "God, my heart is honest and upright before You. To the very best of my ability, I will walk uprightly before You."

Another important principle regarding finances is budgeting and controlled spending. Budgeting helps you control your spending impulses and takes away the pressure and worry about where the money is going to come from for the things that you need.

Some people have never sat down and prioritized the way they pay their bills. Larry Burkett, a Christian financial advisor and consultant, has a little formula that I think is helpful. He says you should take all of your bills when they come in and put each one in an envelope. Then write checks for each one and put these in the envelopes. Put them in order according to the due dates, and mail them at the appropriate times. That's all there is to budgeting. It's setting in order what needs to be paid, and then you know exactly where you are for that month. This way you won't be short at the end of the month because you blew the money you needed for paying bills.

If you don't pay your bills, you're robbing someone. Cindy and I learned a long time ago that if you pay your bills, people like to see you coming. A while back, a bank made an error and withdrew a sizable amount from our checking account—*twice*. Unaware of the transactions, Cindy wrote a couple of checks to the grocery store, and the checks bounced. So I called the bank and had them write a letter of apology to the grocery stores, stating that it was the bank's fault, not ours. We're honest. So we don't go around bouncing checks, and we want the people we deal with to know that. If you're the kind of person who pays your bills, people like to see you coming into their store, because they know you're conscientious about taking care of your financial obligations.

Many men often become defensive if they believe someone perceives them as poor providers. A woman may nitpick her husband for not making enough money, when the guy is out there beating his brains out, doing his best to provide. His self-worth shouldn't be gauged on how much money he's making, but on the fact that he's diligently working to make it. When a woman insinuates that her husband is a poor provider, she is demeaning him and destroying his self-worth. Invariably, this results in either rage or the silent treatment, which are good indicators that such complaining is not a wise thing to do.

If it seems there isn't enough money to go around right now, go back and check to see if you can cut corners on little extras. Instead of telling your husband, "You're not making enough money," say, "Oh, honey, I know you're doing everything you can, and I believe things will get better." Eventually he may feel a drive to work harder because he realizes your acceptance and he will desire to provide for you.

Many times men feel as if they are losing control, and they plunge their families into debt by trying to stay in control. They will go out and buy brand-new cars, knowing they don't have enough money to pay for them. Ladies, this is a weakness. But just love them and help them work through their insecurities. Let them know how unnecessary it is for them to do that to impress you.

Men should understand some needs their wives may have when it comes to finances. Wives are usually interested in the long-term. They like to feel secure about their financial futures. So it's important for husbands to understand that investing and using finances to provide long-term security gives women a deeper sense of security than just providing the quick fixes.

a time to plant, a time to reap

Giving also breaks the spirit of stinginess. One of the greatest and most necessary principles for a family is to sow into the kingdom of God.

> But this I say, He which soweth sparingly shall reap also sparingly; and he which soweth bountifully shall reap also bountifully.
>
> 2 Corinthians 9:6

Again, when you sow, you're planting a seed. But you can do one of two things with seed. You can take it, grind it into meal, make a cornbread cake and eat it—and that's the end of it. Or you can plant that seed and watch it grow and produce more corn; then keep a portion to plant again and eat the rest. That's exactly how it should work with sowing into the kingdom of God. You should hold out that portion that belongs to God, plant it and then eat the rest. Your seed is your tithe. It is 10 percent of everything the family brings home. Eat the balance after the tithe, but don't eat your seed. If you eat your seed, you'll only enjoy it once—and then it will all be gone. Planting, sowing and reaping are part of the necessary process if a family is to walk in financial success.

To achieve financial success in your home, you must have the right attitude concerning money, and you must be willing to plant seed. A home that is willing to plant into the kingdom of God is a home that will begin to prosper. Then the husband and wife will stop being stingy and fighting over the checkbook.

When you tithe, you walk in God's blessings instead of curses. Jesus bore our curses by literally being made a curse for us. (See Galatians 3:13.) Because of His provision, we no longer have to experience the curses of sin and death. Instead, we can walk in God's blessings. Families can walk in blessings in their finances if they cooperate with the plan of God.

> If ye will not hear, and will not lay it to heart, to give glory unto my name, saith the Lord of hosts, I will even send a curse upon you, and I will curse your blessings: yea, I have cursed them already, because ye do not lay it to heart.
>
> **Malachi 2:2**

> Will a man rob God? Yet ye have robbed me. But ye say, Wherein have we robbed thee? In tithes and offerings. Ye are cursed with a curse: for ye have robbed me, even this whole nation. Bring ye all the tithes into the storehouse, that there may be meat in mine house, and prove me now herewith, saith the Lord of hosts, if I will not open you the windows of heaven, and pour you out a blessing, that there shall not be room enough to receive it.
>
> **Malachi 3:8-10**

You have to meditate on and think about the Word of God if you're going to walk in God's financial blessings. You must keep His Word in Your heart and act upon it if you want to find freedom from the curse and live in the blessings. And one way to receive financial blessing is by giving according to the Word of God. Giving with an open heart and a right attitude breaks the cursed spirit of stinginess and greed mentioned in Malachi, which will ultimately produce rivalry between husbands and wives.

believing is doing

We understand the soul of a person to be their mind, will and emotions. As your mind is being renewed in the Word of God and you become a doer, believing and acting upon it, your soul will prosper. And as you act upon the Word in faith, there is a corresponding action from God in response. That's what faith produces—the corresponding action of God.

Now, two of the areas where God wants to release that corresponding action is in prosperity and in health. John says, **Beloved, I wish above all things that thou mayest prosper and be in health, even as thy soul prospereth** (3 John 2). This verse verifies that God wants you to have prosperity and health, but it also indicates that the condition of your soul has a direct bearing on these blessings. We see that when you read the Word and spend time in prayer, God responds by prospering your soul. And as a result, you will be blessed with prosperity and health in your family. God wants you to prosper and have a healthy, victorious Christian family. The devil will always try to weaken your faith, rob you of your inheritance and kill you through sickness or disease. But the important key is that your soul prospers, thanks to Christ's sacrifice on the cross.

what Jesus taught about prosperity

God doesn't expect us to live on the other side of the tracks—He expects us to *own* the tracks. When you say the word *prosper,* some people immediately associate it with being a multimillionaire. Although God certainly can and does cause men and women to be blessed with this type of wealth, that's not what *prosper* means. To prosper means to have total provision or to have more than enough.

Total provision means if you only needed ten dollars to live on and you had fifteen dollars, you'd be rich. The God we serve is El Shaddai, the Almighty One. He is Jehovah-Jireh, our Provider. And He's Jehovah-Rapha, our Healer. He's Jehovah-Shalom, our Peace.

> **But seek ye first the kingdom of God, and his righteousness; and all these things shall be added unto you.**
>
> **Matthew 6:33**

Seeking first the kingdom of God is the key. That means you should seek the kingdom of God first in everything you do—in your family relationship, in your church, on your job, in the way you conduct yourself and in the way you handle your finances. You can't seek wealth in the kingdom of God first. You must seek the kingdom of God first, and wealth will follow.

> **Lay not up for yourselves treasures upon earth, where moth and rust doth corrupt, and where thieves break through and steal: But lay up for yourselves treasures in heaven, where neither moth nor rust doth corrupt, and where thieves do not break through nor steal: For where your treasure is, there will your heart be also. The light of the body is the eye: if therefore thine eye be single, thy whole body shall be full of light. But if thine eye be evil, thy whole body shall be**

full of darkness. If therefore the light that is in thee be darkness, how great is that darkness!

No man can serve two masters: for either he will hate the one, and love the other; or else he will hold to the one, and despise the other. You cannot serve God and mammon.

Matthew 6:19-24

These words of Jesus don't suggest that we *shouldn't* be wise about our finances. And of course they don't teach greed or stinginess. Neither do they suggest that we shouldn't have a savings account or an insurance policy. In this passage Jesus teaches all men and women to put His work on earth first. You can't serve God and money, Jesus says, because giving and greed are incompatible. Christian families should be giving families who seek the kingdom of God first with regard to their finances. If you're going to walk in financial prosperity, you can't walk in deception at the same time. When you make a decision to obey the Word of God because you believe and trust in the kingdom of God, you don't just accidentally wind up with the blessings of God. In actively seeking the will of the One who blesses you, you release the hand of God to open the windows of heaven and pour out His blessings in the Spirit and the natural.

Many people have amassed small fortunes through slavery to their jobs their entire lives. They have large savings accounts; yet when they have a need or it is time to retire, they're afraid to dip into their reserves. They have sizable amounts of money, but they're still poor because they live in fear of running out of money. The fact is that they don't have savings accounts—savings accounts have them. What good does it do to have a million dollars in the bank if you're afraid to touch it?

you can't serve God and money

It is a spiritual fact that men and women who are greedy for money can't serve God. Whatever you place your focus upon first determines what you will receive. If your focus is on Jesus and the kingdom of light, then your eye will be full of the light of Christ, and that light will shine in every area of your life, including your finances. But if money is your god, you will stumble in the dark.

There are several meanings in Greek for the word *mammon*. One word is *confidence* or *trust*.[2] Matthew 6:24 deals with trust and money. Mammon and money are synonymous, but the actual word for *mammon* is the word *trust*. So God says you can't serve Him and put your trust in money, because if you are trusting money, you're going to do things that will disrupt the flow of money in your household. If your trust is in your money and not in God's provision, you'll start serving money and denying God. But when you place your confidence in God, your soul prospers. As you trust God and put His kingdom first, goodness and mercy begin to follow you, and all other material things of life are added to you.

God gives us what we can handle, and that includes money. But our society says, "Get everything right now." Greed says, "I want everything right now. Give it to me today."

When I was in business, I discovered that when my focus was on making money, I seemed to run people off. But when I put God first, I started enjoying my business and received a new level of respect from people.

> **Therefore I say unto you, Take no thought for your life.**
>
> Matthew 6:25

This verse doesn't mean that we shouldn't make plans—it means we shouldn't worry or be fearful. One thing I have learned is that planning always releases you from the fear of tomorrow. When you plan properly according to the Word, you don't just roll with the punches—you establish the path of tomorrow. Planning produces security, and budgeting is part of planning.

gain is not godliness

In 1 Timothy 6, the last part of verse 5 says, **...supposing that gain is godliness: from such withdraw thyself.**

Let me say that gain is not godliness. I believe in prosperity, and I walk in the covenant promises of God, which include giving and receiving. But gain is not godliness unless that gain comes because you have sought the kingdom of God. Someone can gain financially through illegal channels or obtain wealth without earning it. That's why many times lottery winners and gamblers lose their money—and sometimes their families—within a year or two. They come to value money more than people in their lives, and they don't know how to handle the money because it came too easily. They didn't work to earn it, so they don't really appreciate it.

It's important that your attitude and motives stay right between you and God, especially with regard to money. If you want your family to be victorious, there is nothing more valuable than having a quality relationship with God, your spouse and your children. Money needs to never separate you from your family. Don't allow that snare to come into your life. If you put the love of money at the top of your list and spend all of your time trying to get it, you won't be happy, because money can't produce happiness. Money should only be a tool used by God to enhance happiness.

Let me show you what happens when someone is deceived by the love of money.

Moreover the word of the Lord came unto me, saying, Son of man, take up a lamentation upon the king of Tyrus, and say unto him, Thus saith the Lord God; Thou sealest up the sum, full of wisdom, and perfect in beauty. Thou hast been in Eden the garden of God; every precious stone was thy covering, the sardius, topaz, and the diamond, the beryl, the onyx, and the jasper, the sapphire, the emerald, and the carbuncle, and gold: the workmanship of thy tabrets and of thy pipes was prepared in thee in the day that thou wast created. Thou art the anointed cherub that covereth; and I have set thee so: thou wast upon the holy mountain of God; thou hast walked up and down in the midst of the stones of fire. Thou wast perfect in thy ways from the day that thou wast created, till iniquity was found in thee. By the multitude of thy merchandise they have filled the midst of thee with violence, and thou hast sinned: therefore I will cast thee as profane out of thy mountain of God: and I will destroy thee, O covering cherub, from the midst of the stones of fire. Thine heart was lifted up because of thy beauty, thou hast corrupted thy wisdom by reason of thy brightness: I will cast thee to the ground, I will lay thee before kings.

Ezekiel 28:11-17

This passage of Ezekiel is a prophetic utterance with regard to Lucifer, or Satan. He is called the king of Tyrus, but he is literally Satan.

Iniquity was found in Satan by the multitude of his merchants—diamonds, gold and all of the precious stones. First Timothy 6:10 says, **For the love of money is the root of all evil: which while some coveted after, they have erred from the faith, and pierced themselves through with many sorrows.** So the root of all evil is not money—it is the *love* of money. We see this by what happened to Lucifer. He began to love things instead of loving God, and it resulted in his fall.

The love of money is rooted deep in the kingdom of darkness and produces violence, hatred, lying, greediness, stinginess and rejection—which ultimately break up many families. If you fall in love with money, you'll fall out of love with God—and you will err from the faith. So in concluding this vital section of our marriage lifeline teachings, every couple must know that money is a tool to be used. It can be a tremendous servant—but it can also be a horrible master. When we put God first in our homes and businesses, when we bring Him the firstfruits of our labor, He will prosper our lives spiritually and financially. When we commit everything we do to the work of His kingdom, we will prosper from His hand, and there will be no sorrow added to it. (Prov. 10:22.)

Part IV

The Ministry
of a Family

developing a strong family

Once upon a time, a man's word was his bond, ladies acted like ladies and children responded to adults with a "Yes, ma'am," or "Yes, sir." But that was yesterday; today people need legal, binding contracts before entering into an agreement. Not only that, but some women today act like men (and vice versa). And most children have total disregard for authority. Too often the "norm" is to raise kids to be kids, instead of training them to be mature, responsible adults. Children need to grow up emotionally, socially and spiritually. Godly parents who invest time in properly training their children not only create strong families, but they also help build stable environments that have a positive effect on society.

> **That our sons may be as plants grown up in their youth; that our daughters may be as corner stones, polished after the similitude of a palace.**
>
> **Psalm 144:12**

To build a strong covenant-keeping family, you must raise your children to become mature adults. One school of thought says you rob your children of their childhoods when you expect them to become mature and responsible. That's nonsense. Of course, a child should enjoy his childhood, but he should also learn responsibility. Children should be taught to verbally acknowledge someone when they're asked a question, instead of just grunting. A simple "Yes, Ma'am," or "No, Sir" will do. But such manners must begin with the parents. If the parents don't give polite responses and show respect to their own elders, why should their children be expected to act any differently?

If you don't raise your children to act in a mature manner, that childlike behavior will be set in them for life. They may grow up physically, but they will remain immature children living in adult bodies. When things don't go their way at twenty-five or when they get fired or quit their jobs at thirty, they will blame everyone else for everything that is going wrong. They will never learn to take responsibility, develop into maturity or put their hands to something and accomplish it.

a palace vs. a thatched hut

As parents, we need to take great care in how we are building our children. There's a difference between a palace and a wooden building. A palace is well-defined and put together with exactness and precision. It's not just thrown together like a thatched hut. So we need to be exact in the training of our children. The Word says our sons should be mature and our daughters should be polished like stones that fit in a palace.

As Cindy pointed out in an earlier chapter, Paul said in Titus 2:3-5 that the older women should teach the younger women to love their husbands and take care of their homes. Whether you're a natural mother or not, you have a responsibility to influence the younger girls you are around, teaching them to grow up to be godly women. As older and wiser women, you have been entrusted with a most valuable gift—the lives of future women.

As Christians, God has placed us in positions of authority. Whether it is through teaching, preaching, being a big sister or brother or just loving a lonely child, we can influence and instruct children in the ways of God. As a covenant child of God, you are accountable to a great degree for the spiritual, psychological and emotional makeup of the children in your realm of influence. As an adult, you have a part in whether the structure becomes a palace or remains a grass hut.

If we begin early in the lives of our children teaching biblical principles, they will grow up respecting members of the opposite sex and when they marry, they will have respect for their spouses.

one big, happy family

Every household has a personality of its own that is determined by the character of each of the individual family members. Each person contributes something to the atmosphere of the home. Christian families should be strongly knit families with godly atmospheres. Although this may sound idealistic to some, it's not impossible to attain. Even if you're a single parent, you have the God-given right to set the spiritual tone of your home. You don't have to give in to the mentality that one parent is missing and, therefore, your family is lacking in some way. Of course, it's harder for you than for the parents in a dual-parent household, but God promised He would never leave you or forsake you. (See Hebrews 13:5.)

Sometimes you can walk into a house and immediately sense the strife, contention and discord. You know right away the family is unbalanced, because of the evil looks and the catty, snide remarks going back and forth. Let's face it: It doesn't usually take deep spiritual discernment to figure that out. Then there are those homes where the minute you walk past the frame of the door, you sense the presence of the Holy Spirit. Right away, you recognize that it's a home where peace and joy abound. I believe peace is the number one thing God wants you to have in your household.

A strong family is a witness to the world both in word and deed. Look at Psalm 147:19-20: **He sheweth his word unto Jacob, his statutes and his judgments unto Israel. He hath not dealt so with any nation: and as for his judgments, they have not known them. Praise ye the Lord.**

Did you know your family showcases the glory of God? You don't have to be a pastor to do that. We all reflect the glory of God because we're in the body of Christ.

We ought to be families who testify about the Word of God everywhere we go. If you're not going to say something positive about God, then at least don't say something that tears Him down. The words that come out of your mouth should bring glory to God. Don't tear down the kingdom of God with one conversation, then try to stitch it back together with another. Of course, there are times when you're not in a position to verbally witness, because it's not the proper place or time. But when you do have a chance to say something, let it be something that edifies and builds up the kingdom of God. You can live for God every moment of the day, and your family can be a great witness for God without saying a word.

So do you want one big, happy family? It's a process that will take a lifetime to complete. Here are four areas that will help bring it about: forgiveness, fairness, honesty and prayer.

forgiveness

If you're going to have a happy home, you will want to remember and use these important words: "Will you forgive me?" "I'm sorry," and "I forgive you." Families that don't forgive are hurting and unhappy families.

> **The Lord is gracious, and full of compassion; slow to anger, and of great mercy. The Lord is good to all: and his tender mercies are over all his works. All thy works shall praise thee, O Lord; and thy saints shall bless thee.**
> **Psalm 145:8-10**

The word *gracious* means "willing to forgive."[1] God is gracious to us, which means He is forgiving. He's willing to forgive and forget the offenses of our past. And if you're going to have a happy home, one of the first things you should do is make a commitment to let bygones be bygones. Quit trying to stack on top of today all of yesterday's problems. The moment you hold on to any kind of offense, big or small, you start destroying a happy home.

Forgiveness is not always easy, especially in those families who have been touched by the tragedy of divorce. The biggest conflicts arise in blended families where stepparents are involved. This is where you need an extra measure of God's grace and mercy.

Any spouse who brings children from a previous marriage into a new marriage brings added responsibility. The children have to adapt to the stepmother or stepfather, the adult has to adapt to the stepchildren and both parents have to try to blend the two families. So, when tempers are flaring and patience is wearing thin, remember the example set by Jesus—and forgive.

> **Then came Peter to him, and said, Lord, how oft shall my brother sin against me, and I forgive him? till seven times? Jesus saith unto him, I say not unto thee, Until seven times: but, Until seventy times seven.**
> **Matthew 18:21,22**

Before we ever said, "Jesus, will You forgive me?" Jesus had already made a commitment and carried it out. By the same token, we must be people of forgiveness. We must forgive and not link together yesterday's offenses with today's problems. Often after a serious fight, family members ask for forgiveness, kiss and make up, and everybody is happy—until the next day. Then something ruffles the feathers a bit and the first thing out of the mouth is, "I knew it. You did the same thing again—just as you've been doing for the last four weeks." Remember those two killer words, *always* and *never*? When we say our loved ones are "always" doing this or "never" doing that, we make no room for present-day forgiveness.

Remember, your children will eventually leave the nest, and then it will be just the two of you. So, in light of our short lifespan, forgiveness doesn't seem like such a difficult thing, does it? Ask yourself whether the cause you're fighting for today is the battlefield you want to die on tomorrow.

Whether the children are "yours, mine or ours," learn the art of forgiveness. It will save your marriage and your family. Never forget, you're not perfect either. You will have to make a decision to redirect the way you think and talk if you're going to have a strong family, because everybody, at some point in life, will do something that's disagreeable to you.

fairness

If you're going to have a covenant-keeping family, treat each family member equally. Be good to all. You can't have favorites or pick and choose whom you're going to treat nicely. I understand as well as anybody that there are some children you may have a stronger attachment to because of their personalities. But you must make a decision that you're going to love every person in your family equally. Nothing hurts a child more than to see a parent choose his sibling over him. Children have keen sensitivity, and they can pick up on favoritism whether the parent is obvious about it or not. So teach your family to be fair through your example.

While we lived at home with my parents, there were seven of us—five boys and two girls. Not one time was I ever allowed to fight with one of my brothers or sisters. My parents forbade it. If one of my brothers started to hit me and I said something back, my mother would say, "There are enough things to fight about in this life without your fighting one another. If you start that, I'll get my belt and I will calm this down."

A covenant family should learn what it means to serve one another. So we teach our daughters to serve one another. I don't allow any attitudes such as "She never did anything for me, so why should I serve her?"

Husbands and wives can have the same problems. The wife can be sitting there reading a book, and as the husband walks through the kitchen, she asks, "Honey, would you bring me a glass of tea?"

"What's the matter, old woman? Are your legs broken? What's the matter with you, huh?"

Instead, his response should be, "Sure, and can I bring you a cookie to go with it?"

By giving to one another, we serve and love one another.

honesty

The third quality found in a covenant family is truth. Covenant family members don't compromise the Word of God, and they keep the truth forever.

When a couple is dating, both partners will do everything within their power to hide the truth of who they really are.

All their faults, bad habits and negative traits remain hidden because they want to put their best foot forward. But then they get married, and the shiny suit of armor tarnishes. They fall into the daily routine of life, and all those weak areas start surfacing. So the best plan is to be honest from day one so there will be no need to worry about any major surprises later.

Parents, don't lie to your children. The minute you lie to them, you can be sure they'll figure it out. When they're young they think you're almost a god. They think everything you say is infallible, but soon they grow up and have minds of their own. And the moment they realize you lied to them, they will assume they have the liberty to lie too, with justification.

If you can't tell your children the truth, don't tell them anything. If you can't give them a good answer, don't give them just any answer to get them off your back. Sit down with them and talk. The least you can say is "I don't know. Let Daddy look at it. Let Mom see. We'll find out before it's over."

Husbands and wives, never lie to your spouse. Love is built on trust and truth, and a house is built on wisdom. Never allow extended family members-in-law, brothers, sisters, aunts or uncles to put you in a compromising position with your spouse. If a family member talks to you about your spouse and then tells you not to say anything, let that person know there are no secrets between the two of you. Give the devil no place. If other family members have a problem with your spouse, they need to work it out with your spouse—not with you.

Don't allow your own children to compromise the truth between the two of you. If one of your children is in a serious predicament and comes to you, let that child know that he has two parents and that you won't withhold anything from your spouse. You won't lose the trust of the child if you explain that the other parent cares just as much for him as you do.

Secrets between parents and spouses are trust-busters in the family, so guard your family against dishonesty and deception.

prayer

The fourth quality of a covenant family is prayer. You may say, "Well, I'm in this bad situation. I've missed God, and our family isn't doing well. It doesn't look like there's any way out." Listen, it may not look like faith is there, but if you can muster up faith the size of a grain of mustard seed, God will have mercy on you.

When you pray with your children, pray quality prayers. Don't just pray, "Now I lay me down to sleep; I pray the Lord my soul to keep. If I should die before I wake, I pray the Lord my soul to take. God bless Mama, Daddy, us three, maybe four, no more, amen." Instead, pray, "God, I thank You that You've raised us up to take the gospel of Jesus to our generation and that You're going to use our lives to help set many other people free. We ask You, O God, to bless the governor, my school teacher and especially Mom and Dad."

Pray for a hedge around your home, and plead the blood of Jesus over your family. The blood of Jesus is powerful. The Bible says it's His blood that cleanses us from sin. You may have a child or a spouse in a wayward position, but plead the blood over them every day. Don't lose your faith.

Finally, pray in the Spirit. There should be peace within our borders. You can disagree with each other gracefully and tactfully but still keep the peace. There's plenty of violence out in the world, but you can decide not to have it inside your home.

raising children God's way

Let's talk a little more about children now. For those of you who don't have children yet, get ready for one wild ride. If you thought your spouse was unpredictable, wait until the children come along! Children are a gift from God, but they're also a lot of hard work. Remember, though, God doesn't give us more than we can handle. If He blessed you with children, then you *can* handle them.

> **Children, obey your parents in the Lord: for this is right. Honour thy father and mother; which is the first commandment with promise; That it may be well with thee, and thou mayest live long on the earth. And, ye fathers, provoke not your children to wrath: but bring them up in the nurture and admonition of the Lord.**
>
> **Ephesians 6:1-4**

Lesson number one: The greatest way you can love your children is to love their mother or their father in front of them—to honor and bless your spouse. Your children aren't going to do what you *tell* them to do when they get older in life. They're going to do what they *see* you do. It's difficult for children to obey their parents if Dad doesn't love Mom and if Mom doesn't respect Dad.

You can force them to obey you right now, but when they go off on their own, they're going to repeat what they saw while they were growing up. So when they see you walk up to your wife, put your arms around her, kiss her and say, "Honey, you're the most beautiful woman in the whole world"—it makes a lasting impression on them.

When you correct your children, don't correct them to the point of frustration. Correct them to the point of dealing with the problem; then love and bless them. When it's all over, pray with them, instruct them after the correction is over and don't bring it up again. Put it behind you from that point on.

When you speak to your children, always remain consistent in what you say to them. Don't tell them, "We're not going to listen to rock music in this house," and then say yes when they ask you if they can watch MTV. Don't say it's okay, even if it's only for five minutes. Children are very smart, and they will find a million reasons why they don't have to obey you. And they can almost make you believe them. If it's time for them to go to bed, and they're suddenly curious about why the sky is blue or how stars are formed, stick to your guns and don't flounder on the house rules. Let your *yea* be *yea* and your *nay* be *nay*.

When they ask a question, don't put them off—give them an answer. That's one way they know you are in control. If you don't know the answer or you're too busy, say, "I'll tell you what, let me finish what I'm doing and then I'll tell you why it rains." Then run to your encyclopedia, open it up and try to figure out why it rains! When you get back to them, sit down and tell them what you know. You don't have to answer all of the deep questions of life—just take the time to talk to them.

Let your children know they are accepted based upon who they are, not upon their performance. Affirm them verbally, because that's how you love your children, by talking *to* them *about them,* not by talking to them about their accomplishments. There are things my children can't do physically, but I'll never tell them they can't.

Children learn by example, so be careful to be a good one. That's exactly what Jesus of Nazareth did for us—He became our example by showing us how to walk out this life in a human body.

Now Cindy is going to add some more of her motherly wisdom to this discussion. So get ready again to hear from my covenant gift.

"do you know where your children are?"
child rearing
by cindy hallam

Back in the seventies, certain television stations around the nation ran announcements that said, "It's ten o'clock; do you know where your children are?" That was a time when many parents took the time to care and made it their business to know where their children were. But today, the society we live in is so corrupt that we depend on law enforcement to keep our kids off the streets. What happened? Where did we go wrong?

As parents, it's necessary for us to know where our children are, both physically and emotionally. This is more applicable to parents of teenagers because of the worldly ideas and peer pressures that come their way today. As they try to determine on their own what's right and what's wrong, sometimes it leads to poor judgments and they can begin to stray away from the truth. So if we as their parents don't have tight-knit relationships with them, before we realize it, we will have lost them.

Sometimes our involvement in other areas, including ministry, keeps us too busy, and we tend to neglect the care and responsibility for our kids. When they feel we don't have time to deal with their problems or to answer their questions, they find other ways to deal with them—like turning to other people who will give them the attention they need. And this often results in a wedge being forced between the parents and the children.

So as parents, we need to make sure that our first priority is our children and the home God has given to us. And making sure all of you are involved in the same activities is one way to achieve that.

When your children want to spend the night at a friend's house, you need to know what goes on in that household. If you don't know or you have your doubts, don't let them go. Sometimes it's difficult to tell your children, "I'm sorry, but you can't go. We don't know these people, and we don't know what they believe. So until we get to know them better, we don't think it's a good idea for you to stay there." They won't always understand, but that's not the important issue. What's important is what they may be subjected to in that home—on TV, in speech, in ideas and in beliefs. Do the principles and rules of that home coincide with what they learn in their own home and in the church? If not, it will conflict with your teachings as a parent and pull your children away from you emotionally.

Joseph and Mary experienced many of the same parental pressures we experience today. Remember, Jesus wasn't their only child—they had other children after their marriage. And Jesus left an example that is a good pattern for children today.

Now his parents went to Jerusalem every year at the feast of the passover. And when he was twelve years old, they went up to Jerusalem after the custom of the feast. And when they had fulfilled the days, as they returned, the child Jesus tarried behind in Jerusalem; and Joseph and his mother knew not of it. But they, supposing him to have been in the company, went a day's journey; and they sought him among their kinsfolk and acquaintance. And when they found him not, they turned back again to Jerusalem, seeking him. And it came to pass, that after three days they found him in the temple, sitting in the midst of the doctors, both hearing them, and asking them questions. And all that heard him were astonished at his understanding and answers. And when they saw him, they were amazed: and his mother said unto him, Son, why hast thou thus dealt with us? behold, thy father and I have sought thee sorrowing. And he said unto them, How is it that ye sought me? wist ye not that I must be about my Father's business? And they understood not the saying which he spake unto them. And he went down with them, and came to Nazareth, and was subject

unto them: but his mother kept all these sayings in her heart. And Jesus increased in wisdom and stature, and in favour with God and man.

Luke 2:41-52

As Jesus grew, He increased in wisdom, stature and favor with both God and man. But He was still subject to His earthly parents, Joseph and Mary. God gave all children a standard to live by in this world. If any child is going to increase in wisdom, stature and favor with God and man, it will happen because he or she is in the right place—in subjection to his or her parents.

Perhaps you feel like a failure because you didn't follow godly principles when your children were growing up, and now you think it's too late. On the contrary, it's never too late, and there is always hope in every situation. Don't give up just because you messed up!

When Joseph and Mary lost contact with Jesus, it took them an entire day to retrace their steps to relocate Him. We have to be willing to spend the time that's necessary retracing the steps back through life's journey to the point where we lost contact with our children. Maybe it means not going out with friends at a particular time. When we realize our children have strayed from that central focus of the home, we need to be willing to go after them and give them the nurturing they need.

You are the one who is primarily responsible for training that child—not other teachers or men and women in the church—and that may mean a little more work on your part.

There are some things you can do to ensure that the lines of communication with your children remain open—and the most important thing is to talk to them daily, even if they don't like it. As teenagers, they may want their space, but spend time talking to them anyway, pressing through those barriers. Give them as much space as you feel they need, but make sure they understand that the door of communication is always open. Become involved with their extracurricular activities. As busy as we are, we make time to go to our girls' away games. Because we get home late, we lose some sleep, but we make the sacrifice because we love them and want them to know we care.

Know your children's friends. Don't assume because their friends attend church that everything is okay. People from all different walks of life and different spiritual levels come and go in the body of Christ. It's your responsibility to know the lifestyle their friends lead before letting your children become too involved. This isn't being rude, insensitive or snobbish, but it is simply being responsible for making sure your children aren't subjected to anything that contradicts your beliefs and standards.

Correct your children in love when they're wrong, and don't be too intimidated to correct them. Even Jesus was corrected by His parents. Joseph and Mary guided Jesus through His growing years. They let Him know that He was in subjection to them as His earthly parents, and they made sure He was getting everything He needed as a young boy growing up. So follow their leading. Guide your children in righteousness. They need your direction and will always be grateful.

There may be times when your children are afraid, embarrassed or ashamed to tell you something for whatever reason. God will reveal those things to you as a parent if you will diligently pray over your children. The Bible talks about things that are done in secret coming to light. (1 Cor. 4:5.) The Spirit of God will reveal things to you before they take root in your child's life so you can deal with these issues before they ever become problems. That's why it's important to pray continually, not just when you are in the middle of a disaster. Pray that the steps of your children will be ordered of the Lord every day. Pray that God will speak to their hearts and that they will be bold and stand up for righteousness.

Grandparents, you can get in on this too. Pray blessings over those grandchildren. There is something special about a grandparent's blessing that encompasses the entire family. The book of Deuteronomy speaks of blessings and curses. And just as curses extend to the third and fourth generations, so do blessings.

Genesis 17:1-8 talks about the covenant blessing that God promised to Abraham, "to his seed and his seed after him." That extends all the way to us, so freely and confidently speak those blessings over your children. Jacob saw the responsibility to bless his grandchildren as a privilege and laid his hands on them in faith, knowing that God would bless their lives. (See Genesis 48:14.)

children: flowers in the garden of life

Avid gardeners know all the hard work that goes into creating a garden, but they also know the delight in watching the plants and flowers bloom and grow. All the hard work pales in comparison to the reward of watching the garden grow. Children are like a garden. They need to be cultivated, nourished, weeded of bad influences and given space to grow.

As your children begin to grow, make sure they have received the water of the Word. The Word of God provides nourishment to their souls, then washes out the impurities of life and provides them with the essential ingredients for covenant living.

Just as certain minerals are placed in the ground when you have a garden, children need the nutrients of the Holy Ghost in their lives, because the Bible says God wants a godly seed.

Another way you nourish and cultivate your children is with attention and affection. Make direct eye contact with your children when you talk to them; you will find that it places confidence in them when they are considered worthy enough to be attentively heard by an adult. Don't shrug them off, but let them know you value their ideas and thoughts.

Just as you pull weeds which will choke the life out of a growing plant, you may need to "weed" some things out of your children's lives. Many times they will sprout a "crab" grass attitude. You need to weed out sloppy habits and disrespect. If one of my children back-talks one of our teachers, and I find about it, you'd better believe I'm going to do some weeding. There *will* be an attitude adjustment! The Bible talks about how wheat and tares grow side by side and that when a tare first begins to grow next to a stalk of wheat, they look exactly alike. Only the very trained eye can tell the difference in wheat and a tare—until fruit-bearing time. But when it's time to produce fruit, the mystery ends. One produces wheat, and the other produces some kind of worthless weed seed. So ask God to help you discern those things or people that can choke the godly life out of your children.

We can't say this enough: If you're going to have godly seed, you must train by *example*. Children don't always do what you *say*, but they always do what you *do*, because they learn by observation more than by hearing. So if you don't want your child to curse you, make sure you don't curse anyone.

Be there for your children, moms and dads. Guide them. And if you ever happen to lose contact with them, find them and start again. It's never too late when the power of God's Spirit and His love are working through you. Raising godly children is not easy, but with God's help, you can make your garden grow and watch it blossom!

turning hearts toward home

> He shall turn the heart of the fathers to the children, and the heart of the children to their fathers, lest I come and smite the earth with a curse.
>
> Malachi 4:6

The Bible says children who don't love their fathers and mothers have a curse upon them. (See Ephesians 6.) And love is reciprocal. So, one way to turn the heart of a child toward the father is by love.

> Children, obey your parents in the Lord: for this is right. Honour thy father and mother; which is the first commandment with promise; That it may be well with thee, and thou mayest live long on the earth.
>
> Ephesians 6:1-3

The first covenant commandment with a promise in the New Testament is to honor your mother and father that your days may be long upon the earth. So we must teach our children to honor and obey. That doesn't mean we must obey our mothers and fathers all our lives. But even if our parents aren't believers, we can honor them.

Many parents say they don't want to interfere with spiritual decisions. That's ridiculous. You force them to eat green beans and spinach. You force them to take baths and wash their hair. You force them to get out of bed and go to school, and you require that they pass their classes. The truth of the matter is that many parents don't fully believe in the Lord Jesus themselves. So the statement that says "When they're old enough, we'll let them make their own decision" is bogus because you've already made that decision for them. They're observing you, so when they find out you're not committed to God, then they won't be either. Remember, that little child of yours is going to grow up to be just like you one day.

Children don't raise themselves, so it's up to you to bring them up. You can't just give up on raising them because you're tired and you think they'll straighten up when they're older. By the time they're old enough, they've already established the wrong patterns—and it's very difficult to break them. By the time they reach their teens it's very hard for them to change. Only Jesus can intervene in their lives, if they open up to Him.

An undisciplined child is destined for problems, and ultimately, someone with authority is going to intersect his or her path, because we were all made to walk under authority. Every person is under the authority of God, regardless of his or her stature in life. We also walk under the authority of our parents, the coach, the principal, the boss, the president, the sheriff, the mayor—there are many forms of authority in this life.

As a parent, you should be the principal authority in your child's life. But if you don't establish that authority in love, someone else with authority will, and your child will follow him or her. This is why Paul warned:

Fathers, provoke not your children to wrath: but
bring them up in the nurture and admonition of the Lord.

Ephesians 6:4

children don't come with a set of instructions

Unlike your lawnmower, your computer or many other items, children don't come with a set of instructions. But there is a guideline—the Bible. The Word of God says:

Train up a child in the way he should go: and when
he is old, he will not depart from it.

Proverbs 22:6

Learn to discipline in love early. Your children should never be allowed to throw temper tantrums. Perhaps you say, "I'm afraid they won't love me." I guarantee you, they won't love you if you don't discipline them; it's just a matter of time. When little Johnny is three years old and he pitches a fit, he's cute—but when he's thirteen, he's pretty tough to handle. And when he's twenty-three, he's beating his wife because you didn't do what God told you to do.

Don't ever hit your child in the face or on the back. That's not discipline. Those are fits of rage and anger on your part. If you have to discipline your child physically, God made a place to discipline them called the *bottom,* and that's the right place for it.

As we've said, when you teach, you speak. But when you train, it's another level of instruction, and sometimes you must fit discipline into your lesson plan.

Every child has a will of his or her own. If you don't believe this, think back to the moment when your child was born. What's the first thing he did? He started screaming! You will find out very quickly that your children have wills of their own, and there's nothing wrong with that. I personally don't believe you should break a child's will. But I am convinced you should firmly mold it.

Your child doesn't have the right to tell you what to do. You have a commandment from God to train him in how he should live this life and to raise him in the nurture and the admonition of the Lord. And one way you nurture is by correcting him—literally disciplining him to the point of action. Sometimes you must take action with your child to show him your love, because a child will never love someone he doesn't respect.

Some children can be corrected one time and never need correction in that area again. Thank God for them! The point is, don't look for reasons to correct your children, but if the reasons present themselves, never shirk that responsibility of a godly parent in the training of your children.

You may learn how to weave your way around their temper tantrums, little looks and smirks. You may want to give up and say, "It's easier to let them do it than it is to correct them."

The problem is, you program bad behavior into them when you allow that, and when they get out in society, they will act exactly that same way. And by then it will be very evident that they haven't been properly disciplined. Humans are social beings, so we must learn how to function in society, and it starts in the home.

When you discipline your children, you train them in self-control and single-mindedness. You train them to control their emotions, fears, doubts, inhibitions, inferiorities and other complexities that come into their lives. When you require that they work *through* those things, according to God's standards, you guarantee that they will have developed an overcoming lifestyle when they leave home. You'll know that when life dangles the "big carrot" in front of them later on, they can push through the hindrances of the enemy and move into what God has for them.

the switch theory

I had the privilege of growing up in a large family of seven children—five boys and two girls—and our mother believed in the "switch" theory. Some of you are thinking, *A light switch? What do you do with a light switch?* No, Mom would come to church with a switch—a thin, flexible branch or twig that, under the right conditions, could really set us straight. There would be no disrespect for the things of God or other people in our blessed little army.

Parents, never allow your children to curse you. Even if they saw it on TV and turn right around and try it on you, I recommend very strongly that you nip it in the bud right on the spot. The Bible speaks of our current generation that knows no respect:

There is a generation that curseth their father, and doth not bless their mother. There is a generation that are pure in their own eyes, and yet is not washed from their filthiness. There is a generation, O how lofty are their eyes! and their eyelids are lifted up. There is a generation, whose teeth are as swords, and their jaw teeth as knives, to devour the poor from off the earth, and the needy from among men.

Proverbs 30:11-14

Yet God still commands us to honor our parents—it's one of the Ten Commandments. So require honor from your children—never allow them to have a spirit of disrespect.

Sometimes children will be disrespectful in public because they think they can get away with it there. As soon as you sit down in a restaurant, they start acting like they belong to somebody else—and so do you. "I don't know whose child that is throwing guacamole on the wall. I'm going to get up and go to the restroom. When they clean it up, I'll be back."

You can't allow your child to act like that, but there is a proper way to handle it—so here's what to do.

First of all, don't spank your children in public. You will only provoke, embarrass and shame them. Take them by the hand and lead them out of the restaurant—either outside, to your car or into the restroom. Then, correct them there. And when Johnny finishes crying, walk him right back to the table and sit down. People will wonder what you said to straighten him out; they will be amazed because you nurtured him.

Some people come to church and forget they have children. The next thing you know, their children are wildly running around the church, and the ushers are breaking their necks trying to keep up with them. Church is not a playground. Train your children to love the house of God and respect it. Don't let your children run wild. When you train your children to love the house of God, they will learn to worship and praise God openly.

Also, instruct your children that their bodies are the temple of the Holy Ghost, and tell them that until they get married no one has a right to their bodies except them and Jesus.

I once heard a story of a preacher who had two daughters and a son. When each of them reached the age of thirteen, he would take him or her out to his or her favorite restaurant. There he would talk openly and frankly with them about sex, explaining everything and answering any questions they would ask. At the close of the evening, he would open his coat pocket, take out a promise ring and say, "Give me your right hand." Then he would slip the ring on the ring finger of their right hand and say, "Now, this is a covenant. Understand that your body belongs to Jesus, and you will wear this ring in purity until you marry someday."

I thought, *That's wonderful!* Can you imagine the impact that must have had on those children, causing them to want to be holy and virtuous? Children are not a nuisance—they are gifts from God. And they need encouragement to turn their hearts toward a place of acceptance.

turning the hearts of the fathers

According to Malachi 4:6, one of the signs that God has visited the earth is His turning of the hearts of fathers to their children and the hearts of the children toward their fathers.

Now, I have discovered in life that many parents don't like children. To me, that's the most inconceivable thing. I mean, I can't imagine not loving one of our daughters. But in the spirit of the age today, many things are more important to parents than their children.

What is your heart fixed on today? Many parents' hearts are fixed on money, and they consider their children an inconvenient expense. Children aren't an expense—they are wonderful investments in life! Children don't cost—they pay. But if your heart is hooked to your hip pocket, your children will be a nuisance to you every time they need something. Children are gifts from heaven, and one of the overriding abilities of the Holy Ghost is to turn the hearts of parents to their children.

Your children didn't just show up one day; they came because God intended for them to produce joy and bring you pleasure. The joy of a parent is his or her child. But children also came into being because God has a plan and a purpose for them.

Children are extensions of their parents, and they need both mothers and fathers to grow mentally, emotionally, physically and spiritually. I know there are other circumstances sometimes, but the will of God is that the heart of the father be turned toward his children. I am convinced the reason the very first commandment God gave humanity—to have children—

was that there is character development that will never take place in a man or woman until he or she raises children.

Children are gifts of life. At the very moment of conception, on a microscopic level, there's a heartbeat. You can find blood in a tiny child that was conceived only eight days earlier. That child forms with all of its parts intact, and there's life inside of that womb. The moment a baby is conceived, God gives that child a covenant. (See Genesis 9:9.) Now, that child must accept God's covenant when he reaches the age of accountability, and that age varies according to the maturity level of the child.

God expects you as a parent to focus your heart on your children, not on your job, your bank account, your hobbies or simply on your own flesh. Economic conditions can change overnight, and your job may completely shut down. But how do you replace the lost hours that you should have spent with your own family? Some of you have children who are already grown and gone, and there's anger and animosity between you. But be encouraged—the Holy Spirit wants to turn your heart back toward your children. And He will when you ask for His help.

When parents and children aren't in unity, the earth literally bears a curse. Right now, the world is involved in the same sin as Sodom and Gomorrah was. Except for the grace of God, we would be judged as Sodom and Gomorrah was. It is only the blood of Jesus that keeps judgment from falling. Any society that abuses its children, doesn't treat children as a gift from God and doesn't train them to understand the commandments of God has a curse upon it. But, thank God, He's getting ready to reverse the curse!

I have wonderful parents who lovingly taught me to love and honor them. I remember when I was about fourteen years old how I became upset because my dad wouldn't let me do what I wanted. So I went to my room, sulking and having a pity party. I didn't dare talk back to him, because I knew judgment would fall on me if I did. I had been lying on my bed for about thirty minutes, when all of a sudden the door swung wide open, and my dad—six-foot-two and about 230 pounds—walked into that room and said, "Son, I want to know what's on your mind right now."

"Nothing," I mumbled.

Then he looked at me and said, "I'm telling you, you're not leaving this house. You're not running away."

And that's exactly what I was thinking. I was pouting and thinking about how I could run away from home, go to work for a grocery store, play football in the afternoon and come home to my own apartment—all on two dollars an hour. I had it all thought out—I could make $100 a week, $400 a month, and I could get an apartment for $100 a month. Boy, did I think I was sharp.

But dad broke up my little pity party. "Son, I'm telling you right now, until you're eighteen years old, you're not leaving this house. And if you walk out the door with a wrong attitude, I will go out behind you and drag you right back in. Your mother and I love you, and you're going to do what's right."

Dad broke my heart. All I could say was, "Well, that's what I was thinking, Daddy."

His words were burned indelibly into the tablets of my heart. And they've been there ever since, like one of the commandments: "Commandment Number Eleven: Thou shalt not leave home early."

Fathers, turn your hearts toward your children by not provoking them to anger. When you provoke your children to wrath and they reach their breaking point, they will cross the parental line of authority. And once they cross over, it's very hard for them to turn back.

Another way to win your children's hearts is to offer them stability. Children like stability because by nature they are unstable. The moment they're born, they start groping for their mother immediately, and they'll cry out at four in the morning for no other reason than to hear her voice. The moment they hear her voice or find that little blanket, they go right back to sleep—and she's up for the rest of the night!

The most stabilizing factor in any child's life is the relationship they observe between a mother and a father. Husbands and wives, don't just love one another for your own sakes. The love relationship that you show to one another in your home is literally a calming, stabilizing and reassuring factor in the psyche of your children.

Children also need some degree of predictability, and they need routine. Your children need to be able to predict what Mom and Dad are going to do. My children know on Sunday morning that there are no options—we get out of bed and go to church. There's confidence that comes to children when they have a routine that Mom and Dad have established. They need to know what you declare to be right and what you declare to be wrong.

That leads me to the next point: security. Moms, if you can stay home with your children, especially while they're young, I strongly recommend that you do. I know that sometimes financial and living conditions make that impossible, and please don't feel guilty if that is the case. But if you can, stay home with your children.

Finally, covenant parents, if you're going to turn your hearts to your children in your covenant homes, be willing to sacrifice for them. You must be willing to sacrifice your time and your own personal desires if you want your children to be successful and blessed.

As parents you must be willing to surrender your children to the will of God for their future. Don't try to live your desires through them and clone them to be like you, because your children aren't *you*. Be willing to surrender them to their own covenants with God, and let them go when it's time for them to leave the nest. Raising your children according to God's plan prepares them to go out into the world and make their own way. And when the time comes, you let them go, confident that God will honor His covenant concerning them. He will guide and keep them and will turn their thoughts toward the godly home and example you provided for them.

So, let's be all we can be as God's special people today. Husbands, dwell with that fine piece of china God gifted you with as a fellow heir with Christ. Wives, be the needed beam of support for your husband that God fashioned you from Adam's side to be. And, both of you, work together to train up your children in the love and admonition of the Lord. As I think about our earthly homes and all the wonderful memories we hold dear, I'm reminded of our home in heaven and all that awaits us there. Oh, friend, when I look around me and realize that we are living in the last days on this earth, it causes my heart to turn toward my heavenly home! In the meantime, let's allow heaven to dwell in our homes on earth.

endnotes

Chapter 1
[1] Strong, "Greek," entry #5293, p. 75.

Chapter 2
[1] Strong, "Hebrew," entry #1692, p. 29.
[2] Strong, "Hebrew," entry #1121, p. 21.

Chapter 3
[1] Strong, "Hebrew," entry #6763, p. 100.
[2] Strong, "Hebrew," entry #3939, p. 60.
[3] *Mirriam-Webster's Collegiate Dictionary*, p. 1038.

Chapter 4
[1] Strong, "Greek," entry #2961, p. 45.
[2] Strong, "Hebrew," entry #1692, p. 29.

Chapter 6
[1] Strong, "Hebrew," entry #2428, p. 39.
[2] Strong, "Hebrew," entry #2706, p. 42.
[3] Strong, "Greek," entry #391, p. 11.
[4] Strong, "Greek," entry #5293, p. 75.

Chapter 9
[1] Malz, pp. 17-18.
[2] Strong, "Greek," entry #5093, p. 72.
[3] Strong, "Greek," entry #283, p. 10.
[4] Strong, "Greek," entry #591, p. 14.
[5] Strong, "Greek," entry #2133, p. 33.
[6] Strong, "Greek," entry #1411, p. 24.
[7] Strong, "Greek," entry #650, p. 15.
[8] Strong, "Greek," entry #4859, p. 68.

Chapter 10
[1] Strong, "Greek," entry #3126, p. 46.

Chapter 11
[1] Strong, "Hebrew," entry #2587, p. 41.

References

Malz, Betty. *Making Your Husband Feel Loved.* Lake Mary, FL: Creation House, 1997.

Mirriam-Webster's Collegiate Dictionary, 1998.

Strong, James. *Strong's Exhaustive Concordance of the Bible.* "Hebrew and Chaldee Dictionary," "Greek Dictionary of the New Testament." Nashville: Abingdon, 1890.

About the Author

Growing up as the son of a pastor in east Texas, **Walter Hallam** has been active in ministry since childhood. By his mid-twenties, he had achieved a high degree of business success but knew he could no longer ignore the call that God had placed on his life at a young age. In 1985, he and his wife, Cindy, felt led to begin a church in Galveston County, Texas. Abundant Life Christian Center was established in March of that year.

Thirteen years later, with over 3,000 members, ALCC has become one of the fastest growing churches in the nation. Since the inception, Pastor Hallam knew that God was establishing several avenues of ministry at ALCC. These ministries include Abundant Life Christian School (ALCS) with over 350 students in kindergarten through twelfth grade; Abundant Life School of Ministry (ALSOM), which provides intensive training for over 150 Bible school students each year; Abundant Life Ministries of National Destiny (ALMOND), which serves as an International Missions/Ministerial Fellowship; and Abundant Life Evangelistic Media Ministry (ALEMM), which is reaching the world through books, tapes and multimedia ministry, including WIN-TV.

Walter Hallam Ministries is taking the gospel throughout the world today in church services, crusades, print, radio and television. He is currently ministering on over 1,200 television stations in more than 100 nations. Many books and tapes are being published in several languages and are now being distributed by Harrison House, Pneuma Life and others. WORLD IMPACT NETWORK, the latest adventure, involves the television broadcasts "Impact Today," "Abundant Life Today" and "Bethlehem and Beyond," telecasted on Holy Land Television.

Pastor Hallam says resolutely, "I am more excited than ever at the opportunity we have to reach every person on earth with the gospel of Jesus Christ, and I am committed to doing everything I can, with God's anointing and guidance, to be a part of reaching our generation for Him!"

To contact Walter Hallam,
write:

Walter Hallam Ministries
P. O. Box 1515
LaMarque, Texas 77568

*Please include your prayer requests
and comments when you write.*

Additional copies of this book
are available from your local bookstore.

HARRISON HOUSE
Tulsa, Oklahoma 74153

The Harrison House Vision

Proclaiming the truth and the power
Of the Gospel of Jesus Christ
With excellence;
Challenging Christians to
Live victoriously,
Grow spiritually,
Know God intimately.